The
SELF-ESTEEM
Workbook

Judy Bartkowiak

Meet the author

Judy Bartkowiak runs a therapy practice offering one-to-one NLP therapy and workshops from her home in Burnham in Buckinghamshire. Judy is a qualified NLP Business Practitioner, Sports Practitioner, Kids Practitioner, Master Practitioner and NLP Trainer. She trained with Sue Knight in 2001, then with Gemma Bailey and Jeremy Lazarus, returning to Sue Knight for her trainer's training in 2011. Judy is the author of *Be a happier parent with NLP* and the *Engaging NLP* series of workbooks, which are for parents, children, tweens, teens, new mums, returners to work, teachers and people at work.

While her four children were young, Judy ran a Montessori School from home and then returned to working freelance as a children's market researcher before deciding to focus on NLP and writing. She writes children's fiction under the pen name JudyBee. She is also working on a novel and extending the *Engaging NLP* series. Judy is a keen sportswoman and enjoys tennis, hockey, skiing and swimming.

Teach Yourself®

The SELF-ESTEEM Workbook

Judy Bartkowiak

Contents

Introduction

Before we embark on Chapter 1, let's just clarify what we mean by self-esteem and what might be deemed low and high self-esteem. We'll then look at how self-esteem changes and what brings about these changes. Then you'll get the chance to assess your own self-esteem in different areas of your life and set yourself goals as to what you'd like to achieve by the end of the book. And yes, you will achieve your goals!

You will also be introduced to a couple of key concepts that will be covered in more detail later in the book; they are included here to stimulate your thoughts early on as to what benefits there might have been for you in having low self-esteem. Perhaps you'd not thought there might be a positive side?

Let me also suggest to you that in writing this book I am making some fairly fundamental assumptions about you, the reader, namely that:

▶ Having bought a book on self-esteem, you recognize that this is what you want more of and that you are prepared to have a go.

▶ You believe it is achievable.

▶ You believe you are worth it.

▶ You believe you can achieve it for yourself with the help of this workbook.

▶ You are willing to take part in the exercises and be honest in your responses to the questions.

▶ You want to learn how to be different and are prepared to make different choices and change your behaviour.

- You recognize self-esteem in other people; that means you have the wherewithal to have it for yourself as you recognize the elements that constitute it.

- You will, by the end of this book, accept yourself as a truly worthwhile and wonderful person and you can handle this.

→ What is self-esteem?

Self-esteem is the extent to which you feel you are OK, a valuable person in your own right. It is a measure of the opinion you have of yourself in all respects: your physical appearance, how well you perform in your work and sport, whether you feel you are popular and get on with people you meet and how well things are going for you at home with your family.

Only you are the judge of your self-esteem, no-one else can make it greater or smaller. When you lack self-esteem, no amount of well-meaning flattery will change this feeling unless you believe it to be true for yourself. Have you ever experienced this: someone says to you, 'I would have said you were very confident', and you think 'you're so wrong'?

Self-esteem is a feeling and it can change throughout the day, or over a week, month or year. You may be someone who measures it through what you see and the images in your mind; via what you say and how you say it; by your inner voice and how you feel in yourself; or through your actions. However you assess it though, self-esteem is not tangible. It is not a fact and cannot be proven, yet it can affect your sense of well-being and of who you are in the world.

You cannot measure anyone else's self-esteem. In fact, someone who seems very successful and confident to you may actually be feeling very different inside and have low self-esteem, despite being very experienced at hiding it from others.

Here are some of the feelings and thoughts you might experience when you feel low self-esteem.

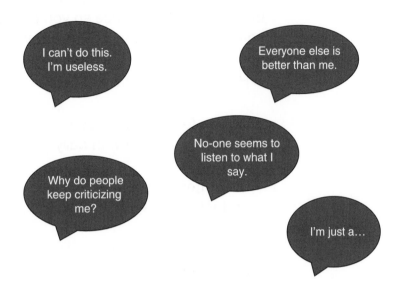

Here are some typical thoughts you may experience when you feel high self-esteem.

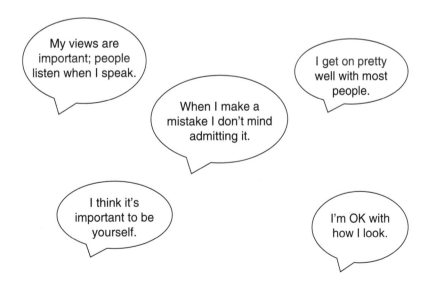

Exercise 1

Here are some questions to ask yourself and think about. You might find it helpful to put a score out of ten in the box after each sentence so you can look at them after you've read the book to see how you have changed.

→ How well do you take criticism? ☐

→ Do you feel valued by your colleagues or those you interact with daily? ☐

→ How often do you say what you really think or do you just agree with the majority view? ☐

→ Do you get what you want from your relationships? ☐

→ Do you take it personally when someone doesn't agree with you? ☐

→ Are you envious of what others have and think they're doing better than you? ☐

→ Do you sometimes feel unloved? ☐

→ Do you feel embarrassed about your appearance? ☐

→ Do you sometimes feel like a victim? ☐

→ Do you feel you're not good enough? ☐

From this exercise, you might find that there are aspects of your life that you haven't thought about before, or words you don't usually use, or phrases that make you think differently. Take a moment to consider these and make a note of your thoughts. Be curious so that you can notice when they occur in your daily life. We will be tackling this later in the book so now is a good time to bring these thoughts to your conscious mind and be ready to make changes for the positive.

THE HIGHS AND LOWS

It's quite normal to go through one day on a rollercoaster of highs and lows of self-esteem. You may wake up refreshed and feel ready for anything (high), miss the train or be stuck in a traffic hold-up making you late for an important meeting (low), but you contribute very effectively (high) and others compliment you on your creative solutions (higher still). Then later you get a call from a difficult client which you don't handle as well as you'd like (low), and you snap at your assistant (low) and realize you still need to finish a presentation your colleague has asked you for today (low). And so it goes on, doesn't it?

Whatever job you are in, whether you work for yourself or whether you aren't in paid work at the moment, life can be a series of ups and downs in terms of esteem.

This rollercoaster effect can be even more pronounced during women's menstrual cycle, menopause and childbirth, but men too can have periods of low self-esteem in their life, sometimes called the mid-life crisis or male menopause but also during times of extreme stress, such as redundancy or unemployment and bankruptcy. Lots of people also experience this rollercoaster in bereavement.

Start to become aware of your own pattern and learn to recognize your own highs and lows. This means that you will be alert to them in others too, enabling you to be sensitive to their needs and know how to help. However, this book is not about helping others; it is about how you can help yourself and thereby become a model that others can learn from.

Exercise 2

Keep a diary of your day to keep track of when you experience high and low self-esteem. There isn't a typical day really is there? So think about yesterday as it will be fresh in your mind. Notice the balance of highs and lows.

Time of day	Is my self-esteem high or low? Score out of 10.	What happened? What was the factor that caused you to give it that score?	Has this happened before, is it a pattern?

What do you notice in this exercise? What are the patterns? How could you change the pattern by doing something different? Diet and exercise both affect our sense of well-being, so could you eat or exercise differently to bring about a better state of mind? Lack of sleep or poor sleeping patterns can also lead to less resourceful thoughts and behaviours. Could you change this to effect a positive state?

Are you affected by what you see, what you hear or by something someone does at a particular time of day that you could change so you respond more positively?

You can experience highs and lows of confidence even at different points during an event. Here's an example.

Case study

Beth was very nervous when her boss Simon asked her to present at their next sales conference. She immediately felt sick and thought about how she might get out of it (low). She even tried to persuade Simon that one of her colleagues would be a better choice (lower) and eventually told Simon that she didn't think she'd be able to do it at all because of her nerves (lowest). He asked her some questions about the content of the presentation, which she answered very confidently (high) and he complimented her on her knowledge of the subject and her ability to convey even quite complex concepts that they had been working on (higher). Then he suggested she looked for some amusing or interesting quotes to illustrate what they wanted to say. By the time they met again, Beth was feeling much more confident and she was able to transfer her content into bullet points on cards. After a couple of rehearsals she was good to go!

Beth's presentation started with some initial nerves, sweaty palms and a slight stutter (low), but Simon gave her an encouraging smile (high) and she delivered one of her rehearsed quotes which got a laugh from the audience (higher). From then on it was plain sailing until question time. As the steward came forward with the microphone, she panicked that someone would ask a difficult question (low), but the first questioner praised her on her excellent presentation (high) and asked her a question that she was easily able to answer (higher). She was pleased that everything had gone well (high), but cross with herself for being so nervous about the whole thing (low).

What we focus on, is what we get more of. By focusing on what went well and what is going well in the moment, we get more of it. By ending on low self-esteem Beth will repeat the pattern next time she's asked to give a presentation. She needs to live in the moment and not dwell on what happened in the past.

POSITIVE INTENTION

We are not by nature out to sabotage ourselves deliberately, so why do we allow ourselves to fall into these lows of self-esteem? Could it be that we get some benefit from it? Let's assume we do. At this stage in a book on self-esteem it is important to explore what we get out of our low self-esteem, because if what we get from this behaviour is ultimately of greater value to us than high self-esteem, then we will never successfully conquer it.

Exercise 3

Think of the last few times you experienced low self-esteem and write them below. You will then be invited to consider in an exploratory way what positive result you might have got from having that low self-esteem. Here are some possible reasons for you to consider.

▶ It enabled me to get some attention/sympathy/ affection that I felt I needed.

▶ It enabled me to get out of doing something I didn't want to do.

▶ I was able to stay in my comfort zone.

▶ I appeared braver than I really am.

▶ Other people gave me the support I needed.

Now think about benefits you derive from low self-esteem. What were they and what did you get out of it?

→The time when:

_____

_____

_____

_____

_____

_____

→ On that occasion what do you think you gained from having low self-esteem?

_____

_____

_____

_____

_____

_____

→ The time when:

_____

_____

_____

_____

_____

_____

→ On that occasion what do you think you gained from having low self-esteem?

_____

_____

_____

_____

_____

_____

→The time when:

_____

_____

_____

_____

_____

_____

→On that occasion what do you think you gained from
having low self-esteem?

_____

_____

_____

_____

_____

_____

Was it a surprise when you discovered that there can be
a gain from having low self-esteem? In this book we will
explore how you can get the same positive intention but not
via the low self-esteem route.

Here is an example of how Adam used his low self-esteem.

Case study

Adam was a great skier but not the best in his group of friends. He was certainly strong on the black slopes (the hardest slopes), but when it was icy he found himself getting a bit nervous. His legs would turn to jelly and he'd make a bit of a fuss, suggesting they do another slope first and come back to the icy black or the moguls later in the day once the sun had been on it for a few hours. When he thought about what his positive intention was for this behaviour, he realized that he wanted the others in the group to notice him and appreciate that he was finding it hard so they would encourage him and compliment him when he went down it well.

COMPELLING OUTCOME

Before we get started on the workbook, let's set a compelling outcome. A compelling outcome is a goal or objective which just belongs in that single situation and reflects what you want to achieve from it. How confident do you want to be? How much self-esteem do you want?

Exercise 4

Go back to Exercise 1 and look at your scores. What score would you like to see in each of these boxes? Write in the box the score you want to see there by the time you've read and completed all the exercises in this workbook.

→ How well do you take criticism?

→ Do you feel valued by your colleagues or those you interact with daily?

→ How often do you say what you really think or do you just agree with the majority view? □

→ Do you get what you want from your relationships? □

→ Do you take it personally when someone doesn't agree with you? □

→ Are you envious of what others have and think they're doing better than you? □

→ Do you sometimes feel unloved? □

→ Do you feel embarrassed about your appearance? □

→ Do you sometimes feel like a victim? □

→ Do you feel you're not good enough? □

Thinking about the scores you have recorded above, let's give them a voice by completing the following sentences.

→ When I feel someone is being critical I want to:

_____

_____

_____

_____

_____

➜ I want my colleagues to value me because I:

_____

_____

_____

_____

_____

➜ In future when I disagree with what someone says I will:

_____

_____

_____

_____

_____

➜ I want _____

_____

_____ from my relationships.

➜ When someone disagrees with me I will just think:

_____

_____

_____

_____

_____

→ When I am tempted to feel envious I will remind myself of:

_____

_____

_____

_____

_____

→ When I feel unloved I will remember that:

_____

_____

_____

_____

_____

→ I will make some changes to my appearance in these areas:

_____

_____

_____

_____

_____

→Instead of feeling like a victim I will remind myself that:

_____

_____

_____

_____

→I am good enough because I:

_____

_____

_____

_____

You may have other specific confidence goals so record them below.

→I want to be able to:

_____

_____

_____

_____

→I want to feel:

_____

_____

_____

_____

_____

→Or use your own words:

_____

_____

_____

_____

_____

Self-esteem is how you value yourself and your contribution to your world and those you interact with and whom you care about. Another word for it is self-worth or confidence. The aim of this book is for you to achieve a sense of high self-worth on a consistent basis and at the ecological level – which means that this sense of self-esteem has a positive impact on those around you and is a good example to them.

1 Sources of low self-esteem

- -

In this chapter you will learn:

▶ *How to identify signs of high and low self-esteem*
▶ *Where low self-esteem comes from – because no-one is born with it*
▶ *How your perceptions of yourself may differ from others' perceptions*
▶ *That you have a choice about your self-esteem*

- -

We weren't born with low self-esteem or indeed with self-esteem issues of any kind. Nevertheless, low self-esteem started in the past and we will explore in this chapter how your low self-esteem began and decide whether it still has any place in your life today. You will discover that you have choices about which aspects of your childhood you decide to retain and which you want to dump. Before you do either, you will look at how some negative thought processes have a positive benefit, so let's check yours out and see if we can keep the benefits but lose the low self-esteem?

Let's start by learning how to recognize self-esteem.

Exercise 5

Here are a few questions to ask yourself. Answer honestly now! Tick the boxes that apply to you.

→ Do you often find yourself saying 'yes' when you really want to say 'no'? ☐

→ Do you prioritize other people's needs and leave yours until there's no time left for you? ☐

→ Do you find it difficult to express yourself and sometimes get a bit tongue tied and end up not saying what you meant to say? ☐

→ Do you frequently say 'sorry' even if it wasn't your fault? ☐

→ Do you often feel a failure? ☐

→ Do you ask other people for help making decisions? ☐

→ Do you compare yourself unfavourably with other people? ☐

→ Do you use the phrase 'I can't' quite a lot? ☐

→ Do you hold back from taking chances or opportunities to take the limelight? ☐

→ Do you feel guilty about decisions you have to make? ☐

How many boxes have you ticked? If you have ticked *any* of them you have work to do! This is a good thing though, because now you have brought these behaviours to your conscious mind where you can work on them.

....

All of the above are signs of low self-esteem and we are going to go back through them in the next exercise in order to examine where they came from. These are all patterns you have picked up probably in childhood. They may be patterns you observed and experienced in one of your parents or other significant people in your childhood, such as a teacher or grandparent.

There are a number of factors that contribute to children experiencing low self-esteem and we will look at these afterwards. First let's explore where they came from.

Exercise 6

Write underneath each behaviour who you think has exhibited this behaviour in your past. We are not attributing blame here, simply understanding how the pattern has come about so we can decide what we want to do about it and whether we want to change it now.

→ Who in your childhood used to say 'yes' when they meant 'no'?

_____

→ Who prioritized other people's needs and left theirs until there was no time left for them?

_____

➔ Who used to find it difficult to express themselves and sometimes got a bit tongue tied and ended up not saying what they meant to say?

_____

➔ Who used to say 'sorry' even if it wasn't their fault?

_____

➔ Who used to feel a failure?

_____

➔ Who used to ask other people for help making decisions?

_____

➔ Who used to compare themselves unfavourably with other people?

_____

➔ Who used to use the phrase 'I can't' quite a lot?

_____

➔ Who used to hold back from taking chances or opportunities to take the limelight?

_____

➔ Who used to feel guilty about decisions they had to make?

_____

Have you mentioned the same person in a number of these answers? It has been and still is your choice how you respond to the influences around you, both now and from your past. The people who have influenced you meant well and had a positive intention for you even if it may seem difficult to understand it. You don't have to continue with this pattern yourself. Instead you can make new patterns with the help of this book.

··

Having established whose pattern you have copied, now is the time to decide whether you want to carry on doing that or whether you might want to change it. The pattern may have suited them and may have been appropriate for them at that time, but if it isn't working for you then now's the time to change it. Is this a strange idea? Perhaps it is, but you *can* change beliefs you have about yourself! We'll be working on that in the next chapter.

Let's look at other ways you can develop low self-esteem that might not relate to copied patterns of behaviour, but from how you were brought up. Parenting styles change all the time and parents bring to their own parenting, aspects of how they were brought up which may vary according to their age, culture and experiences.

Case study

My school friend Jan was brought up by fairly liberal 1960s parents and was one of five girls. When her parents divorced, her mother remarried Mark who was understandably fazed by the idea of suddenly becoming a step-parent to five young girls. He was a lot younger and not of the liberal 1960s generation. He went overboard on the discipline and hardly let the girls out of the house. They were very angry of course and rebelled against him. Jan lost all her confidence along with her beautiful hair through developing alopecia.

There are a number of factors in parenting styles that can contribute to low self-esteem in adults.

Focus on the negative

If your parents or teachers/carers noticed what you did wrong or where you fell short of their expectations (which may well have been unrealistic) but didn't praise you for what you did achieve.

High expectations

Some high-achieving parents assume their children will also be brilliant, clever and do well at school, but this is not always the case of course. You might have been excellent in your own, different, way but if it was not what was expected for you it may not have been recognized.

Negative comparisons

When parents or teachers constantly compared you with other brighter pupils or siblings and you felt that you were 'not good enough'.

Neglect

When parents' busy lives and stressful occupations, frequent absences and lack of contact, result in a child not receiving the emotional and physical support they need when growing up.

Abuse

Children who have been physically or verbally abused find it difficult to feel valued.

Being different

If you were very different from your peers or siblings through being from a different culture, or being a different colour, size, religion or having a different temperament, this can lead to feelings of low esteem. Sometimes just wearing glasses, having a stutter or a skin condition can make a child feel different.

These situations do not necessarily lead to low self-esteem. It is not the facts in themselves that create it but your perception of the facts. You can have a biased perception if you think that whatever you do is wrong, or notice the negative responses rather than the positive ones, and this can be the result of a pattern copied from your parents. For example, if a parent constantly puts themselves down or has low self-esteem themselves, their child might look out for situations or experiences that would lead them to the same conclusions. Similarly you can have biased interpretations such that you subconsciously distort the meaning you attach to a situation. For example, if your parents say something positive you still decide that they didn't mean it or were just trying to be nice.

Have you heard of cognitive dissonance? We are familiar with this term perhaps more in a business context for buyer behaviour. We know, for example, that after a buyer has made a purchase, they only notice positive reviews of that brand and selectively dismiss anything negative as being ill-informed. This is the same with self-esteem. Once we have an idea in our head that we are shy, lacking confidence or self-esteem then we notice behaviour that fits that version of ourselves rather than any evidence to the contrary.

It works for high self-esteem too. Are you more likely to notice, for example, a colleague's high self-esteem if you perceive them to be confident and overlook, or not even notice, times when they lack confidence or have low self-esteem?

With this in mind, the next exercise is designed to challenge the view you have of yourself based on the previous exercises.

Exercise 7

Think of the last time you...

➡ Said 'no' when you meant 'no':

_____

_____

_____

_____

_____

_____

_____

_____

➡ Prioritized your own needs:

_____

_____

_____

_____

_____

_____

_____

_____

_____

➜ Expressed yourself well:

_____

_____

_____

_____

_____

_____

_____

_____

➜ Didn't say 'sorry' because it wasn't your fault:

_____

_____

_____

_____

_____

_____

_____

_____

_____

_____

➜ Felt you were a success:

_____

_____

_____

_____

_____

_____

_____

_____

➜ Made a decision by yourself:

_____

_____

_____

_____

_____

→Compared yourself favourably with others:

_____

_____

_____

_____

_____

_____

_____

→Said 'I can do that':

_____

_____

_____

_____

_____

_____

_____

_____

_____

_____

→ Took a chance or an opportunity to take the limelight:

_____

_____

_____

_____

_____

_____

_____

_____

_____

_____

→ Didn't feel guilty about a decision you made:

_____

_____

_____

_____

_____

_____

_____

_____

_____

_____

· ·

You see, you are able to do it! Finding the exception to your usual behaviour pattern shows you that you do have the skills and resources to respond differently. Go back and re-read what you wrote in this exercise and remember how you felt at the time. Now how are you feeling? Write it in the box below.

Can you see that you have choices? You can focus on what you are doing well or you can focus on what you are not doing well. It is your choice. It is about perceptions not facts.

Here's another way of looking at it.

How we see ourselves is not how others see us. Whilst we might feel we have reasons to have low self-esteem, others may see you differently. Their perception of you is different. They may see what you do well and expect you to have high self-esteem. What do your friends and family think of you? In the next exercise you are going to write this down for your partner, friends and parents by ticking the adjectives that you think they would use to describe you. Then you should check with them whether you have got it right and find out what adjectives they would use to describe you that you have not ticked. How many will you have missed out, I wonder?

Exercise 8

I think my partner thinks I am...	Partner: I think he/she is....
Kind	Kind
Funny	Funny
Honest	Honest
Open to new ideas	Open to new ideas
Argumentative	Argumentative
Interesting	Interesting
Clever	Clever
Considerate	Considerate
Good looking	Good looking

Creative	Creative
Sporty	Sporty
Confident	Confident
Affectionate	Affectionate
A good listener	A good listener
Bossy	Bossy

Did this open a 'can of worms'? Where are the similarities and what areas are different? Look at the adjectives you've ticked on behalf of your partner; find out what attributes they notice in you that you have been unaware of until now.

I think my friend thinks I am...	Friend: I think he/she is....
Kind	Kind
Funny	Funny
Honest	Honest
Open to new ideas	Open to new ideas
Argumentative	Argumentative
Interesting	Interesting
Clever	Clever
Considerate	Considerate
Good looking	Good looking
Creative	Creative
Sporty	Sporty
Confident	Confident
Affectionate	Affectionate
A good listener	A good listener
Bossy	Bossy

Friends often have similar personality traits, so if there are qualities you admire in your friend they may also be true of you. Check this with them and find out!

I think my mum/dad thinks I am...	Mum/Dad: I think he/she is....
Kind	Kind
Funny	Funny
Honest	Honest
Open to new ideas	Open to new ideas
Argumentative	Argumentative
Interesting	Interesting
Clever	Clever
Considerate	Considerate
Good looking	Good looking
Creative	Creative
Sporty	Sporty
Confident	Confident
Affectionate	Affectionate
A good listener	A good listener
Bossy	Bossy

As children we were very conscious of when we did not meet our parents' expectations, and parents tend to fill the role of correcting and disciplining for unsatisfactory behaviour. You are an adult now though. Check that this is reflected in your answers above.

....

In order to do the exercise above, you had to put yourself into the shoes of other people, but were you correct?

Comparing the different sets of adjectives, what do you notice?

_____

_____

_____

_____

_____

_____

_____

Of course some of the adjectives may be construed as either positive or negative, and some of them may not be important to you in a particular context. For example, in a work context it may not matter to you whether other people think you are sporty, unless perhaps you are a PE teacher! So now we'll look at how you *do* want other people to think of you.

When people have low self-esteem it is usually because they have a poor sense of self-worth and are possibly only noticing evidence of their low self-worth rather than picking up on evidence to the contrary. They are distorting reality. You may have noticed some distortion of reality in that last exercise, but whose reality matters: your own or other people's?

Your beliefs, like self-confidence, started forming in childhood. Did you have parents who considered it important for you to be confident? Were they confident themselves? How did that manifest itself? What cues signal 'confident' to you? Sometimes it helps for you to think of someone you want to be like in terms of confidence or self-esteem.

Exercise 9

Write down below a description of three people you know who are confident in a way you would like to be and give some examples of what they do, how they look, what they say and any other clues that tell you that they are confident.

Name	What do they do that leads you to the conclusion that they are confident?	How do they look that makes you think they are confident?	What do they say that makes you think they are confident?	What other clues tell you that they are confident?

What patterns do you see? The fact that you can recognize these outward signs of self-esteem suggests that you could copy them and have the potential to be confident yourself. So why don't you?

In many cases people who lack self-esteem continue this pattern because they have a positive pay-off, in other words, there is some benefit to their having low self-esteem. Before you dismiss this as nonsense, consider what that benefit could be, if this were true. Be curious. What possible benefit could there be for you in having this low confidence?

Here are some questions that might help.

Exercise 10

What will you have to do when you are confident that you don't have to do at the moment?

➜ When I am confident I will have to:

_____

➜ What will you no longer be able to do once you are confident that you *can* do now?

_____

➜ When I am confident I won't be able to _____

_____

_____ any more

➜ What do other people do for you that you will be expected to do for yourself when you are confident?

_____

➜ When I am confident I will have to _____

_____

_____ for myself.

Are you prepared to make these changes? Let's start now! Acting as if you are confident already is the first step along the way.

....

Case study

Dan was known to be shy and quiet at work and so he was never asked to make any speeches at people's leaving dos, or stand up and give presentations in meetings. He noticed that he was passed over for promotions that would have suited his capabilities and this made him angry although he never expressed it at work. Whilst he was relieved not to be asked to come out of his comfort zone, and enjoyed taking a back seat, the result was that no-one knew what he was capable of. His pay-off for being shy was beginning to pall as he watched his colleagues being promoted above him.

Of course it is easier to take a back seat and stay in your comfort zone. This is your pay-off, the *benefit* of having low self-esteem. You can stay in your comfort zone and never put yourself to the test. This means you don't set yourself up to fail. However, do you ever feel like Dan and wish you could show your team at work what you can do? How could you get the benefits of staying in your comfort zone and yet achieve higher self-esteem without the down-side of risking failure and embarrassment? What do you think is the answer?

_____

_____

_____

_____

_____

Do you realize that in order to make changes in your life and improve your self-esteem, you do have to step out of your comfort zone. Let's examine this comfort zone of yours. Imagine that your comfort zone is a physical space and you are in it. Believe that through the power of your mind and your imagination you can change all the aspects of your comfort zone just by choosing to do so. Now tick the boxes, as you make the changes, and see whether your comfort zone changes sufficiently to enable you, perhaps even to encourage you, to escape and move on. It may help you to draw a picture of you in your comfort zone before you start. It doesn't matter at all how your picture looks or how well drawn it is.

	Better	Worse	Same
Make the colour lighter	☐	☐	☐
Make it darker	☐	☐	☐
Change it to your favourite colour	☐	☐	☐
Make it larger	☐	☐	☐
Make it smaller	☐	☐	☐
Make it smell lovely	☐	☐	☐
Make it taste lovely	☐	☐	☐
Make it clear and transparent	☐	☐	☐
Make it opaque	☐	☐	☐
Bring it closer	☐	☐	☐
Move it further away	☐	☐	☐
Make it into something you like, e.g. jelly	☐	☐	☐
Give it a lovely tune	☐	☐	☐
Make it quiet	☐	☐	☐

Which changes made a difference? _____

_____

Which changes enabled you to step out of your comfort zone rather than allowing it to keep you trapped and unable to move on for fear that something dreadful

will happen? How does your comfort zone look now?
Draw it below.

```

```

Did you notice the words we used earlier: '**when** you are
confident'? We are assuming you *will* be confident. Do you
share the expectation that you will have higher self-esteem
by the time you've worked through this book?

Yes ☐   No ☐

I hope you have answered 'yes'. If you have answered 'no',
then why is that? In order to have high self-esteem you need
to be able to visualize it and believe it to be both possible
and probable; that you deserve it and are worth it. You will
be doing a great number of exercises in this book designed
to make this possible and probable and to explore the idea
of being 'worth it' and deserving it. For now though, let's
examine your beliefs around self-esteem. What do you
believe will be different when you have high self-esteem?
Presumably you believe that it will be a good thing to have,
otherwise you would not have bought this book! So why is
it a good thing to have?

Exercise 11

What are your beliefs about self-esteem? Complete the following sentences.

➜ People who have high self-esteem are:

_____

_____

_____

➜ It is a good thing to have high self-esteem because:

_____

_____

_____

➜ I will be _____

_____

_____ when I have high self-esteem.

➜ It is good to have high self-esteem because you can:

_____

_____

_____

Self-esteem isn't just a bipolar scale where there is high self-esteem at one end and low self-esteem at the other, and it doesn't always remain the same does it? You may feel confident in one area of your life: maybe you are great at golf or singing or some other skill? Also, when you have to perform at work, give a presentation or discipline one of your employees, you may feel more confident than when you are at a networking event. Our confidence isn't static but moves along a scale between high and low.

Exercise 12

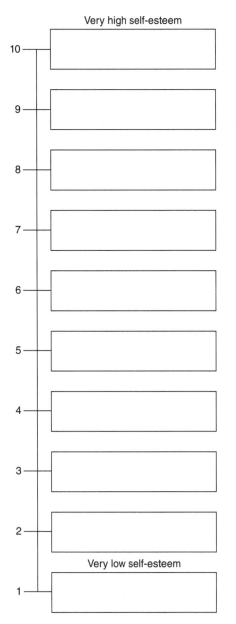

Very high self-esteem

10

9

8

7

6

5

4

3

2

Very low self-esteem

1

Here is your own personal self-esteem scale. Let's assume the score 1 is incredibly low self-esteem and 10 is super high self-esteem. The numbers between relate to the different levels of self-esteem you might feel at different times, in different situations and so on.

Beside each score write down a corresponding situation or issue that relates to that level of self-esteem. Think about *all* aspects of your life. You may surprise yourself to find that you have much higher self-esteem in some areas of your life and much lower self-esteem in other areas.

→ Focus points

▶ Signs of low self-esteem are:

▷ Saying yes when you mean no

▷ Putting other people's needs first

▷ Finding it hard to express yourself

▷ Comparing yourself unfavourably with others

▷ Saying 'I can't' frequently

▷ Tendency to feel guilty

▶ You have the choice whether you want to perpetuate low self-esteem patterns picked up in childhood.

▶ By focusing on occasions when you display high self-esteem you will start to change the pattern.

▶ Other people have a different perception of you. Take this on board!

▶ If you can spot high self-esteem in others you have the ability to have it yourself.

▶ What is the benefit to you of having low self-esteem? How can you get the 'pay-off' without the behaviour?

What have I learned?

→ What signs of low self-esteem will I work on changing?

_____

_____

_____

→ How will other people's perceptions of me enable me to build my self-esteem?

_____

_____

_____

→ How will I become more aware of when I'm in my comfort zone?

_____

_____

_____

→ How will I move out of my comfort zone and increase my self-esteem?

_____

_____

_____

Summary

In this chapter we have looked at your self-esteem, how it manifests itself and how it can change according to your environment. We considered where it had come from and invited you to think about whether now might be a good time to change some of the beliefs you have about yourself in this respect.

You also did an exercise where you put yourself in someone else's shoes and looked at yourself from a disassociated position and considered how others might see you. This is a good thing to do on a regular basis because we can be inclined to associate too much, and just think about how we see ourselves and the world, without considering how others may view the situation. 'The map is not the territory' as we say in NLP (Neuro-Linguistic Programming). The ability to step outside ourselves and look objectively at what we do and how we do it is a big step along the way towards improving our self-esteem.

Where to next?

In the next chapter we are going to focus on your identity and your beliefs and values.

Who we are is influenced by our childhood, age, gender and culture, and we will explore the impact of these on who we are as adults. We will look at how our life experiences and interests affect our identity. How do you define yourself and how did this come about? What really matters to you? The next chapter is intensely personal and cuts to the basics to explore the very essence of who you are.

2

Living according to your values and beliefs

In this chapter you will learn:

▶ *How your childhood has contributed to who you are today*
▶ *How you can reframe negative experiences and extract the learning*
▶ *What is important to you*
▶ *How your beliefs can help or hinder you*

Be yourself and be happy with the person you are. Love yourself and be happy with your identity. In this chapter we explore what matters to you, what you hold to be true and what qualities you want to hang on to as you develop your self-esteem through this book. Self-esteem is about accepting yourself as you are 'warts and all'. There will be things that you think you want to change and we will be working on these throughout the book. There will also be aspects of your identity that you may feel differently about as you read the workbook. First let's look at who you are: your identity.

Exercise 13

WHO ARE YOU?

When students apply for higher education they often have to write a personal statement. Let's do this now. Write your own personal statement, describing yourself, your strengths and weaknesses, what's important to you in life and what makes you special, to impress and wow the reader.

_____

_____

_____

_____

_____

_____

_____

_____

Do you come across as confident and self-assured? Have you included your strengths and skills?

....

Who we are is not so much about the roles we play, what we do for a living or how we spend our time. We are who we are because of how we respond to what we experience. Take a group of people and expose them to the same experience and they will each respond differently. This difference is explained by the fact that we will base our response to events and people on a number of factors such as:

- ▶ Childhood – how we were brought up, where, by whom and in what culture.
- ▶ Our age – different generations grow up with different mores and this will determine to some extent how we view our world.
- ▶ Gender – men and women are different!
- ▶ Experiences – how past experiences have made us the people we are.
- ▶ Values – what we feel is important in life.
- ▶ Beliefs – what we hold to be true about the world.

The influence of our childhood on who we are has been covered to some extent in the last chapter. Our parents' values and beliefs will have been passed on to us both subconsciously and directly in terms of spoken instructions, e.g. 'We don't eat like that' or 'Don't talk when I'm talking'. Our parents in turn will have been influenced by their parents of course.

If you were brought up by one parent, this will have affected you and be different from, say, your partner who may have been brought up by two parents. The area and the cultural environment in which you spent your childhood will affect who you are. One only has to witness two colleagues suddenly discovering they went to the same school or lived in the same town to feel the sense of kinship they have from this shared environment.

In the last chapter we learned how negative parenting can have a lasting effect on us. Here are just a few of the sorts of phrases that could result in us feeling low self-esteem as an adult.

As children we tend to believe adults, especially our parents and teachers. However, if when stretched to their limits or stressed, they say things about you that you remember and believe, these can become your identity.

Equally, if your sibling was, in your perception, the favoured child and you had to do more to win approval and maybe never felt you did, then this can result in a feeling of low self-worth. This sometimes happens if you are the eldest child and find yourself having to grow up rather quickly and help out in the home as opposed to being able to enjoy your childhood. Younger, cuter siblings can tend to take the limelight where the older child has to 'be sensible' or 'act your age'.

In some cultures it is usual for several generations to share a household and this can result in children being effectively brought up by an older generation as perhaps their parents go out to work and they spend more time with grandparents. It can work either way; some grandparents will spoil you and leave parents to do the disciplining but others will have old-fashioned ideas about what children can and can't do and make sure you 'don't get too big for your boots'.

> Case study
>
> I have an Asian friend whom I met when we were students at Kingston Uni on our Post Graduate Diploma in Marketing course. He was an amazingly creative guy, very talented and conscientious. He was very keen to go into advertising and we all encouraged him. However, his family told him that he would never get a job in advertising because he was Asian. So when he had no success he gave up very quickly and followed the path his family expected which was to go into education. He later took a PhD and became Dean of a UK university. His family's belief that Asians don't get jobs in advertising affected his belief about his own possibilities.

Exercise 14

Think about your own childhood for a moment. What aspects of it do you feel affected you?

What factors seem to you to be significant in your up-bringing that you feel have made you the person you are?

	How has this influenced who you are, the type of person you are?	How has this influenced you in your work situation?	How has this influenced you socially?	How has this influenced you in your relationship with your partner?
Your own parents – their upbringing, jobs, income level, marriage, values				
Birth order – are you the eldest, middle, youngest or an only child?				
Upbringing – were your parents strict, laid back, over-protective, critical? Did they have high expectations?				
School experiences – were they positive and enriching? Did you do well or did you feel a failure? Were you popular? Did you excel at certain subjects or at sport, music, drama or art?				

(Continued)

	How has this influenced who you are, the type of person you are?	How has this influenced you in your work situation?	How has this influenced you socially?	How has this influenced you in your relationship with your partner?
Age – how old are you and what life stage are you at now? Where are you along life's path?				
Gender – what kind of a man or woman are you and how does your view of the role of men and women affect your life choices?				
Past experiences – what key events in your life have affected you?				

How we regard these factors, whether we blame them for negative influences or attribute them to our positive ones, can be a matter of perception. Those same influences can be reframed or looked at in a different way. It is obvious that they can be viewed differently because, as mentioned earlier, we all take something different out of the same experience. So how could you reframe any of the factors you've listed so they could be advantageous to you? Could any of them have given you a useful or valuable resource that other people don't have? Imagine it like flipping a coin.

Exercise 15

Inside each of these coins write a belief or value that you feel stems from some aspect of your past that is negative or limiting you in some way. Then write in the flipped coin how you could turn it into a positive belief that you can use to your advantage.

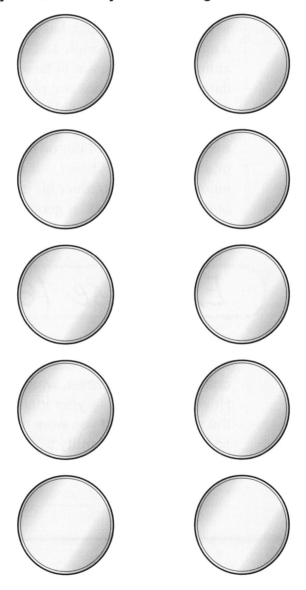

Your age and gender will to some extent influence who you are e.g. 'a child of the 60s' or 'a war baby' or 'a feminist' or 'Thatcher baby': these all relate to the political and social climate of the time you were growing up. It isn't set in stone and there are many people who stand out as not being typical of their generation.

> **Case study**
>
> My Dad is 92 years old, has a laptop as well as a PC, a mobile phone, a Kindle and is altogether very techie although his career was in finance. He is more up to date with both finance and technology than many of my generation, because he holds the belief that it's important to keep up. My brother on the other hand, despises all things techie and will not own an iPod, smartphone or a microwave; his belief is that these technological innovations would reduce his quality of life because outside of work 'slow' is good.

Exercise 16

How do you feel your age and gender affect who you are today? We take these for granted; after all, we can't change them! However, what do those facts give you? How do they add to your identity? You would not be the same person if you were a different age or gender, so what specific identity traits belong to your age and gender?

_____

_____

_____

_____

_____

_____

_____

_____

· ·

Our past experiences mould us into the person we are today, whether we have gone to university, been travelling, owned our own business, been divorced, had children and so on. We will have more in common with others who've done the same things and we'll also have been affected by the experiences, albeit not necessarily the same way. Many people say that such life-changing experiences as, say, having cancer or losing a child, or having a baby, completely change their identity and make them question who they really are, perhaps for the first time.

Exercise 17

What life-changing experiences have you had? What influence has each one had on you? Write down your examples below.

→As a result of _____

_____

_____

_____

_____

→ I am _____

_____

_____

_____

_____

→ As a result of _____

_____

_____

_____

_____

_____

→ I am _____

_____

_____

_____

_____

→ As a result of _____

_____

_____

_____

_____

_____

→I am _____

_____

_____

_____

_____

→As a result of _____

_____

_____

_____

_____

_____

→I am _____

_____

_____

_____

_____

→As a result of _____

_____

_____

_____

_____

_____

➜I am _____

_____

_____

_____

_____

➜As a result of _____

_____

_____

_____

_____

➜I am _____

_____

_____

_____

_____

Have you managed to extract the learning and positive
intention of each life experience?

Our hobbies and interests give us identity, for example, as
an artist or a reader of *Vogue* magazine, a golfer, a pianist,
a gardener. Although how we spend our time doesn't
automatically become our identity, it contributes to it in just
the same way as our occupation.

> Case study
>
> My husband is a geologist by profession but his passion is cycling. His identity is very much as a cyclist and he notices cyclists everywhere: on the street, in films, on TV and so on. He eats as a cyclist, exercises as a cyclist and his view of the world is that of a cyclist. He is many other things, but none define him so precisely.

Exercise 18

Think about your hobbies and pastimes. How do you spend your leisure time or the time not taken up by work? Maybe it would help to think about what you like to do on holiday or how you would spend your ideal weekend or time off work.

Let's start each sentence 'I am a _____'

EXAMPLE 'I am a walker'

➜ I am a _____

➜ I am a _____

➜ I am a _____

➜ I am a _____

➜ I am a _____

➜ I am a _____

➜ I am a _____

➜ I am a _____

→ I am a _____

→ I am a _____

Perhaps, like me, you have been reminded through this exercise that you don't spend enough time doing the things that define you as a person? How could you make more time for yourself to redress this imbalance in your life?

··

Of course work does take up most of our time, although it may not define who we are. For some it will, especially if you have a vocation such as teacher, nurse, doctor and so on. These types of professions are usually associated with commitment over and above the job itself.

Exercise 19

Think about what you do but not in terms of the job title or even the responsibilities: write down the role that most defines you and is most important to you. Sometimes it helps to think about what you would miss most about your job if you were to lose it today.

_____

_____

_____

_____

_____

_____

_____

_____

_____

_____

_____

_____

_____

_____

_____

_____

· ·

These exercises will have given you the opportunity to explore different aspects of your identity and you probably realize how much there is about you that you have taken for granted. This is therefore a good time to consider your values and what is important to you.

Your values are what you would, if you had to (and let's hope you don't!), fight for; those things that are so important to you that you would not compromise them and would under no circumstances give up. They may be things like 'freedom', which is quite general, so in the next exercise be as specific as you can and write down what really matters to you. You are asked for your top 10 so have an eraser to hand in case you change your mind as you work through it.

Exercise 20

These are the things that matter most to me and make me the person I am:

1 _____

2 _____

3 _____

4 _____

5 _____

6 _____

7 _____

8 _____

9 _____

10 _____

How do you feel about them? Any surprises? Write your thoughts below.

_____

_____

_____

_____

_____

_____

_____

_____

_____

_____

_____

_____

_____

_____

· ·

Lastly in this chapter, we will explore beliefs. Beliefs are inclined to change more than values. Whereas your values were probably learned in your childhood, and developed over the years to what they are today, your beliefs may change frequently as you experience new things, talk to new people, travel and read.

As we grow older and become better informed, we adapt our beliefs accordingly. Those beliefs we had in childhood, such as believing in the Tooth Fairy, Father Christmas and that our parents know best, will certainly have changed, along with our religious and political views, social opinions, professional beliefs and personal beliefs about ourselves and those close to us.

You will have numerous beliefs, probably several about any topic one could mention, so there isn't enough room in this book to list them all. Instead we will focus on beliefs about ourselves and what we can and can't do, because it is usually those limiting beliefs (the things we think we can't do) that affect our sense of self-esteem.

Exercise 21

I believe the things I am good at are:

1 _____

2 _____

3 _____

4 _____

5 _____

6 _____

7 _____

8 _____

9 _____

10 _____

I believe the things I am not good at *yet* are:

1 _____ ☐

2 _____ ☐

3 _____ ☐

4 _____ ☐

5 _____ ☐

6 _____ ☐

7 _____ ☐

8 _____ ☐

9 _____ ☐

10 _____ ☐

Note that the word 'yet' has been added because beliefs change.

Taking the things you've listed in the second list, do you believe that you could be good at them all? In other words, do you believe that you can learn how to do them? Go back and put a tick alongside all those you believe you have the possibility to change and be able to do once you learn how.

Now go back and look at what's left. Is there anything left?

Looking at anything you haven't ticked; ask yourself, in the light of all the work you've done on your identity in this chapter, how important is it to you to be able to do this thing, or do you just feel you ought to be able to do it? If you don't actually think it's that important to you then cross it out because you're holding onto someone else's belief that this is important, and that's pointless isn't it?

··

Case study

For a long time I thought I ought to ski down black runs because my friends could do that and they knew I had enough ski-ing ability to do it. I just thought I was pathetic, being scared of going fast and ski-ing down very steep slopes. Then I considered whether it was fundamental to my belief that I loved ski-ing and that I was a good skier for me to do black slopes and I decided it wasn't. Phew! What a relief. I changed my belief and relieved myself of unnecessary low self-esteem in the ski-ing department!

For the remainder of this book try to focus on real self-esteem issues for you and get rid of those issues that belong to other people's beliefs about you and your identity.

To finish this chapter, complete the sentences in the next exercise.

Exercise 22

➜ What I really love about myself is:

_____

_____

_____

➜ I think I'm a really _____

_____

_____ person.

➜ I can see why people love _____

_____

_____ about me.

➜ I contribute _____

_____

_____ to those I come into contact with.

→I inspire other people by my:

_____

_____

_____

→What I really want to keep is my:

_____

_____

_____

→What gives me self-worth is my sense of:

_____

_____

_____

→What I value most about myself is:

_____

_____

_____

→What's really important to me is:

_____

_____

_____

➡ People respect the fact that I:

_____

_____

_____

➡ I know I can develop my self-esteem further because:

_____

_____

_____

Was that difficult? I expect it was. Most of us find it difficult to recognize our good points despite being able to easily spot those of our friends and family. You probably found it became easier as you went through the questions, so go back and take a look at the first few that you answered and see if you can answer them better now.

··

➡ Focus points

▶ Who we are determines how we respond to external events and whether we will demonstrate high or low self-esteem in the managing of them.

▶ The same external event will provoke a different response depending on:
  ▷ Our age and gender
  ▷ Childhood experiences
  ▷ Upbringing
  ▷ Values and beliefs

▶ Self-esteem will be affected by expectations of how we 'should' be.

▶ Our hobbies and interests reveal our values in life and what is important to us. How you spend your time tells others what you place value on.

▶ Beliefs are what you hold to be true about yourself and the world you live in. Is there a belief that by changing it you could improve your self-esteem?

What have I learned?

→ What would impress other people about me?

_____

_____

_____

→ How have my life experiences moulded me into the person I am today?

_____

_____

_____

→ Which of my beliefs could I change to improve my self-esteem?

_____

_____

_____

→ What do I do in my spare time that reflects my identity?

_____

_____

_____

Summary

In this chapter we have explored identity and looked at how your childhood experiences and the roles you play at work and in your social life, and your leisure activities, make an impact on your identity. We looked at values and beliefs and checked whether what you believed about yourself that has been contributing to your self-esteem is really fitted to your values and beliefs about your identity.

Where to next?

One of the most frequent pieces of feedback
I get from NLP workshops is how surprised
people are that behaviours which they thought
were unconscious and unchangeable can in fact
be changed quite easily. By bringing them to
consciousness, you can examine them and decide
whether you want to continue the pattern or not.
In the next chapter we will continue to explore
choices and how flexibility can be so powerful. This
flexibility and ability to manage your mood and
outcomes brings with it the self-esteem you desire.

3 Changes and choices

In this chapter you will learn:

► *How changes and choices you make at one level will impact the others*
► *The importance of alignment towards your purpose in life*
► *That skills you have in one part of your life can be transferred to another*

The person with the most flexibility controls the system. By opening yourself up to more choices through enhanced self-esteem you have the opportunity to change and become the person you want to be. In this chapter you can explore what you want for yourself and what changes and different choices you could make to achieve it.

Becoming the self-assured person you want to be is achieved by becoming aligned, which is a state when you are completely at one with yourself and your environment, behaviour, skills and values.

How do you know when you are aligned? Most people say that they can feel it; they feel different, relaxed and comfortable with themselves and who they are. They also feel confident and have high self-esteem, so let's get cracking on the Logical Levels of Change which was adapted by Robert Dilts from an original model produced by Gregory Bateson.

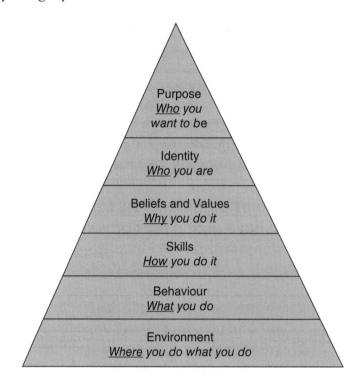

At the top of the pyramid you will see PURPOSE, and it's no surprise it appears at the arrowhead with all the other levels below it because purpose is where we are heading for in life, what we are aiming for and what we'd like to be remembered for when we are gone. This isn't meant to be a morbid thought, but rather what we want people to remember us for, our achievements and what contribution we made to their life. This is a BIG question and one you may want to think about and come back to, but if you can, write in the space below (on the 'gravestone') what you'd like your purpose to be. Doing it quickly now is more likely to give a real representation of your purpose than if you spend ages thinking about what you think it ought to be.

Exercise 23

Write your epitaph on the gravestone below. I know it's a bit spooky, but imagine what you'd like people to say about what you have achieved in life when you are gone, the sort of person you are and what they will remember about you.

The purpose of this exercise is that we all work too hard and have so little time usually for what is important to us. This often leads to frustration and poor self-esteem because we aren't achieving what is important to us. By looking into the future and thinking about how you want to be remembered you have to question your identity, and this is where we go to next.

Now let's take the next level down on the Logical Levels of Change pyramid. This is IDENTITY: it is who you are. Sentences on this level start 'I am...'. Keep in mind what you said your purpose was and ask: so what does that mean I am?

Exercise 24

Without giving this too much thought, write down below the first ten things that come to your mind about who you are. Think about using adjectives to describe who you are, e.g. 'I am sensitive' or nouns 'I am a writer'. There are no right or wrong answers here and you do not need to impress anyone, so just write it how it is and be honest about who you are.

→ I am

_____

→ I am

_____

→ I am

_____

→ I am

_____

→ I am

_____

→ I am

_____

→I am

_____

→I am

_____

→I am

_____

→I am

_____

I expect you've done this quickly because, compared to many of the other exercises, it was quite easy wasn't it? Go back now though and just check whether what you've written actually defines you. If someone you met socially was describing you to someone else, what would they say? What would they remember about you that would stand out? Do these statements make you happy? Do you feel proud of who you are? Do they fit with your purpose?

· ·

To begin the process of alignment, your statements need to be in accord with your purpose. For example, if your purpose is to run a marathon and your identity is a couch potato there is a mismatch which you will need to change! Either you decide you don't want to run a marathon after all or you decide you need to stop being a couch potato and start training for that marathon! If that is the case you need to add to your identity 'in training for a marathon'. In the next exercise you will think about what aspects of your identity need to be in place to fit with your purpose.

Exercise 25

→ In order to achieve my purpose I need to be:

_____

_____

_____

_____

_____

_____

_____

_____

Now how will you achieve this change? Let's move on to your beliefs and values because this is how you'll do it.

....

Beliefs are what you currently hold to be true about the world in which you live. They may relate to religion, politics, your social environment, the role you play at work and at home or indeed any opinion you hold about your life and those you spend time with. Beliefs are constantly changing as we meet new people and learn more about the world. As we travel, read newspapers and books and integrate our new learnings and experiences we reassess our beliefs in line with them.

Some of your beliefs may well stem from childhood and relate to the beliefs passed on to you by your parents, teachers and peers. Perhaps you still hold them to be true for you today. Other beliefs may have been changed as you've grown up and learned more about life through new experiences, or perhaps they've changed because the world itself is different now to how it was when you were a child.

Changing beliefs isn't traumatic. Often you may simply find they've changed without you realizing it. When you need to make a change in one of the Logical Levels you may very well need to look at your beliefs to check whether there is one that is holding you back from making that change. For example, if you believe you are not 'a numbers person' yet the promotion you want requires some aptitude for numbers, you need to rethink that belief and recall times when you had the belief that you need now.

Exercise 26

What beliefs would you like to have now that will move you forward with the purpose you have identified?

➜ I would like to believe:

_____

_____

_____

_____

_____

_____

➜ Have you ever believed this? If you have, when was that?

_____

➜What caused you to change that belief?

_____

➜If you haven't ever had this belief, then what evidence would you need now in order for you to be able to change it?

_____

➜What's stopping you changing this belief?

_____

Sometimes we can find ourselves clinging onto a belief that really has no place in our life and prevents us making progress. This is called a limiting belief. Now is the time to examine beliefs that make it difficult for us to make the changes we want to make in order to achieve our purpose.

➜What could you do right now to change a belief that is getting in your way?

_____

_____

_____

_____

_____

Values are rather different to beliefs in that they tend to be more firmly ingrained and part of our personality. They are what we hold to be irrevocably true for us. They are what runs through our core and make us who we are.

Case study

My father values anything he has to work hard at. Although he is 92, he reads avidly, asks questions, considers problems and strives to find solutions through learning about everything. This enquiring mind is a big part of who he is and always has been. He values learning and places value on what he does not yet know. It is more than a belief, it is unchanging and fundamental to the person he is.

What do you value? What are your values? This exercise will help.

Exercise 27

What do you value? What are your priorities in life? Who and what do you put first?

It is easy to take what we have for granted, but what if some of these things were to be at risk of being taken away? What rights that you currently have would you hate to lose?

1 _____

2 _____

3 _____

4 _____

5 _____

6 _____

7 _____

8 _____

9 _____

10 _____

Isn't it strange how we take things for granted yet many of the things we value in life can be things like clean air to breathe, peace, food on the table, our family, love, friendship and so on. In many parts of the world people don't have these.

These values are unlikely to change with time, although your beliefs may well do so. Looking at your values above, do they accord with the beliefs you hold? Are they aligned?

· ·

Now check your identity level from earlier exercises. Is it aligned with your values? Your values are *why* you do what you do.

Let's look now at *how* you do what you do: your skills and strengths.

What do you do well? Now it's probably fair to say that most people underestimate their strengths, and if you have low self-esteem sometimes then you could be doing just that.

Here is your opportunity to grasp your strengths by the tail and put them in one place where you can access them whenever you need to give yourself a confidence boost.

Exercise 28

What are you good at? Make a list here.

1 _____

2 _____

3 _____

4 _____

5 _____

6 _____

7 _____

8 _____

9 _____

10 _____

How does each of these skills enable you to make the change you want to make? Which skill is going to be the most useful in the process? Think about the skill itself. How exactly do you do that thing? Imagine yourself doing it and be curious about the steps you will take to do it. Write them down here.

1 _____

2 _____

3 _____

4 _____

5 _____

Now think about the underlying belief that you have about that skill. When you do the thing that you do well, what is your belief about the skill?

→ I believe that this skill:

_____

_____

_____

_____

_____

How do you value the skill or the fact that you have and use this skill in your life?

_____

_____

_____

_____

_____

_____

_____

_____

_____

_____

_____

As you know, skills are transferable to other parts of your life. So think about how you use this skill in your work, sport, home life and social life.

➡ I use this skill in my work when I:

_____

➡ I use this skill in my sport when I:

_____

➡ I use this skill in my home life when I:

_____

➡ I use this skill in my social life when I:

_____

· ·

Has this given you some ideas about how you can also transfer this skill and others you've listed, to make the changes you want to make? Write down your ideas in the space below.

_____

_____

_____

_____

_____

_____

_____

_____

_____

_____

_____

_____

_____

Isn't it strange how we tend to shrug off compliments?
Think about what your friends and colleagues say you
do well. Many of our skills we take for granted, because
perhaps we've always done them and think everyone can do
them but this is often not so.

Exercise 29

**What do your friends, family and colleagues say you
do well?**

**Can you write a list of the skills other people say you
have, even if you don't particularly agree with them?**

1 _____

2 _____

3 _____

4 _____

5 _____

6 _____

7 _____

8 _____

9 _____

10 _____

One problem we sometimes experience which holds us back from recognizing our skills is that we compare ourselves with others who are better than us. This is called being externally referenced and is a really good way to reduce your self-esteem. Come on! This is a workbook on improving self-esteem, so be internally referenced and consider the things you believe you do well, even if others may do them better. This is about your PB (personal best) not winning every race!

Case study

The other day I played doubles in tennis with someone I hadn't played before. We won both sets and I played much better than I usually do, although not as well as I used to. My partner complimented me on my game and I thanked her, but inside I told myself that my play wasn't as good as it could be. Why did I do that? I did play well.

Are there some other skills you have forgotten? List them below.

1 _____

2 _____

3 _____

4 _____

5 _____

I wonder what skills you had forgotten. Ask your friends and family, and maybe look at some old photos to remind yourself of all the things you have been able to do in the past and can still do now if you recall the skill.

The next level down on the Logical Levels of Change pyramid is behaviour, or *what* you do. At this level we need to think about all the things you actually do. This is likely to be a very long list. Let's split them into the things you do regularly and the things you do occasionally. You need to include those things you do that you don't enjoy and would rather not do. You also need to include the things you do that you are not proud of.

Things I do regularly	Things I do occasionally

Now we need to think again about the Logical Levels of Change so that we can make changes where we need to in order to be aligned to our purpose.

Looking at your lists above, tick all the things you do that align you to your purpose: they help you achieve what you want to achieve and they are of value to who you are. How many have you ticked?

Give some thought to those things you haven't ticked. Have you heard of the 3Ds?

These are delegate, dump and do.

Delegate the things you *can* delegate and bear in mind and accept that they will not be done as you would do them, but if they are not aligned to your goals then you don't need to do them. You won't be able to delegate all the things that don't fit with who you are and who you want to be, but there will be some that you can, so write DELEGATE alongside those that fall into this category.

Dump the things that don't really need to be done at all and that are taking up time which you could be spending on the things that are important to you. Not everything we do has value to us and not everything we do are things we 'believe' we need to do, so free yourself from time-wasting activities that take you away from what is important to you. How can you have high self-esteem when you don't value your time? Write DUMP alongside those things.

Do the rest! Do the things that matter, that you feel are important and have value to who you are and where you want to go in life. With other things having been delegated or dumped, you now have more time for the 'to do' list. You will have higher self-esteem when you concentrate on what is of value to you. Draw a big circle round those things you plan to do more of and write in the space below what you now have time for that will enable you to make the changes you need to make to fulfil your mission in life.

_____

_____

_____

_____

_____

_____

_____

_____

_____

_____

_____

At the base of the Logical Levels of Change pyramid we have the environment: what you can see, hear, feel and touch. This refers both to your physical environment in terms of where you live, work and play and to your metaphysical environment, which is the culture of where you live. This is where we do what we do. When you make changes higher up the logical levels, you may find that as you start to align yourself by tweaking and changing aspects of what you do, that you need to also adjust your environment in order to be able to do it.

Exercise 30

Let's take a look at your environment. It may help to use all your senses for this. Focus on where you do the thing that relates to your purpose so that you align the relevant environment. So if you want to make a change in your work, think about where you work, and if you want to make a change at home, think about that environment, and so on.

→ What do you see? When you think about your environment what images come to you?

_____

_____

_____

_____

_____

→ What do you hear? What sounds are there?

_____

_____

_____

_____

_____

→ What's the temperature like: is it too hot, too cold, or about right?

_____

_____

_____

_____

_____

→ What about the atmosphere? Do you feel comfortable?

_____

_____

_____

_____

_____

→ What about smell? Is there a good smell or a bad smell?

_____

_____

_____

_____

→ This may not be relevant, but what about taste? Is there any element of taste?

_____

_____

_____

_____

_____

→ How do these elements work for you in terms of being aligned to your goals and purpose? What could you change so that your environment is aligned with what you do, how well you do it, your identity and vision?

_____

_____

_____

_____

_____

_____

· ·

Now let's remind ourselves of the Logical Levels of Change pyramid.

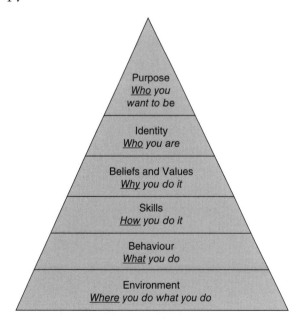

Purpose
Who you
want to be

Identity
Who you are

Beliefs and Values
Why you do it

Skills
How you do it

Behaviour
What you do

Environment
Where you do what you do

Exercise 31

We have worked down the pyramid, so now let's work back up again, having made changes along the way. Note what changes you are going to make at each level in order for you to be aligned to your purpose.

→ My purpose is _____

and the changes I will make are:

→ Environment

_____

_____

_____

_____

_____

_____

_____

→ Behaviour

_____

_____

_____

_____

_____

_____

_____

_____

➜Skills

_____

_____

_____

_____

_____

_____

_____

➜Beliefs and values

_____

_____

_____

_____

_____

_____

_____

_____

➜ Identity

_____

_____

_____

_____

_____

_____

_____

➜ Purpose

_____

_____

_____

_____

_____

_____

_____

Now do the exercise again, this time with the purpose of raising self-esteem.

➜ My purpose is to increase my self-esteem and the changes I will make are:

→ Environment

_____

_____

_____

_____

_____

_____

→ Behaviour

_____

_____

_____

_____

_____

_____

_____

→ Skills

_____

_____

_____

_____

_____

_____

_____

_____

→ Beliefs and values

_____

_____

_____

_____

_____

_____

_____

→ Identity

_____

_____

_____

_____

_____

_____

_____

→ Purpose

_____

_____

_____

_____

_____

_____

_____

_____

By moving fluidly up and down the Logical Levels of Change pyramid, making changes, tweaking, looking at different choices and becoming aligned, you will have developed the skills to use this process constantly whenever you feel out of alignment.

....

When you feel uncomfortable or out of alignment ask yourself:

► At which level do I feel out of alignment?

► What do I need to change at the level above this?

► What do I need to change at the level below it?

► What other levels are affecting this state?

► What do I need to change there?

Then check that all is aligned.

→ Focus points

▶ Self-confidence comes from being aligned: being completely in tune with your environment, values, beliefs, goals and skills.

▶ The Logical Levels of Change is a pyramid, with the environment at its base and purpose at its apex.

▶ The process of alignment is one involving the examination of your life at each level and making changes in order to achieve it.

▶ Start by identifying your purpose, then line up each level in the pyramid so they each support it.

▶ You can choose where you place attention and significance. You can choose to keep things the same or change them.

What have I learned?

→ What are the six Logical Levels of Change?

_____

_____

_____

→ At which level have I had to make the most changes in order to become aligned?

_____

_____

_____

→ What limiting beliefs have I had to challenge?

_____

_____

_____

→ What have I decided to delegate or dump, leaving me more time to 'do'?

_____

_____

_____

Summary

In this chapter we have travelled the six Logical Levels of Change: environment, behaviour, skills, beliefs and values, identity, and purpose, making choices along the way. Flexibility is key to alignment, which is our goal. Skills can be transferred from one part of our life to where we need them to achieve alignment, and limiting beliefs can be changed.

Where to next?

As we set about changing things and making choices, tweaking behaviours and becoming aligned, the one thing that will help us is feedback. In the next chapter you will learn how to turn your own responses and those of other people, both verbal and non-verbal, into learning experiences to act as your rudder for direction during the process.

4

There's no failure, only feedback

In this chapter you will learn:

▶ *To identify how you respond to different types of feedback and how to handle it more resourcefully using techniques such as anchoring*

▶ *That by disassociating and being curious about the positive intention you can reframe the negative feedback into positive learning*

▶ *To use feedback in a positive way as part of your ongoing personal development*

How well do you handle criticism? Do you have a fear of failure? We can get negative feedback at home and at work, verbally and non-verbally. Do you take it as a sign of failure or can you appreciate the positive intention, which is to learn from it and do something different next time? How often do you shrug off positive feedback saying 'it's nothing' without acknowledging the skill and thinking of ways to use it elsewhere in your life?

Exercise 32

Criticism can come in many forms, so let's start this chapter by considering what they are and thinking about how you respond to each. Look at the following types of criticism. After each one, write an example of when you have experienced such a criticism. Then give each situation a score out of ten for how badly you felt about it.

Direct overt verbal criticism

This is when someone criticizes you to your face and there is no question in your mind that it is a criticism, e.g. 'Your report was dreadful.'

_____

_____

_____

_____ ☐

Direct overt written criticism

In this instance the criticism is in written form as a text, email, letter, review or report, e.g. 'You need to rewrite this report as currently it is unreadable.'

_____

_____

_____

_____ ☐

Indirect verbal criticism

When someone criticizes you via a third party, e.g. 'He has a really off-putting manner with clients.'

_____

_____

_____

_____ ☐

Indirect written criticism

The criticism in this case is written about you rather than to you, e.g. 'This book is badly written with lots of grammatical errors and poor punctuation.'

_____

_____

_____

_____ ☐

Direct but covert criticism

Here you are feeling criticized by someone's body language rather than anything they directly say to you. Perhaps they've turned their back on you as you approach or have not spoken to you when you ask them a question. They maybe look at you in a way that implies they don't like you or do not want to be friendly for some reason which is not clear. You may have done something which they show disapproval of by the way they look at you or by looking away.

_____

_____

_____

_____ ☐

Indirect covert criticism

This is the sense we get when we are excluded from a party or meeting, perhaps an event to which others in our peer group have been invited.

_____

_____

_____

_____ ☐

Which did you score highest? Are you more affected by what you hear, what you read or what you feel? In Chapter 5, you will learn much more about what we call VAK – visual, auditory and kinaesthetic. For now, write down here what patterns have you noticed.

_____

_____

_____

_____

_____

_____

_____

_____

··

It isn't the criticism itself that causes us problems is it? It is our response. Our response will vary according to a number of factors:

► Whether you believe it to be true or fair.

► How you are feeling at the time.

► Who is doing the criticizing.

► The tone and the way it is communicated.

There are several ways of handling criticism and by learning all of them you will have an armoury of techniques for different situations.

→ Disassociating

We can associate into a situation, which means that we experience it to the full by totally absorbing ourselves in it. As you can imagine, that's not a great feeling when it comes to criticism! Instead we can disassociate by stepping away from it emotionally and regarding it as if from a distance both physically and emotionally. We can imagine ourselves as an impartial observer experiencing it. We then view, read or hear it as if we are outside the situation, like a 'fly on the wall'. So ask yourself, what would someone else make of this criticism? By distancing yourself in this way you get a more rational response which will probably be more resourceful. From there you can then decide if you think the criticism is fair and make a reasoned response and plan how to manage the next stage, which is rectifying the situation.

→ Anchoring

Anchoring can be used in so many different situations. It is a device for getting us into a resourceful state by associating a physical action, mental picture or a word with how we would prefer to feel. Thus, we can use an anchor when we experience criticism in order to stay calm and unflustered, and also to feel strong and well-placed to consider the learning and pause before making our response. The following exercise shows you how to anchor.

Exercise 33

▶ Step 1. First decide what your anchor will be. It can be an action, such as squeezing your earlobe or putting your thumb and index-finger together like this:

It can be a mental picture, such as imagining yourself in a favourite relaxing place, or visualizing a painting you love that makes you feel good. It could be a piece of music you really enjoy that relaxes you when you hear it. Whatever you decide to use as your anchor for this exercise, practise a few times now before you start so you can access it when you need to.

▶ Step 2. Now think about a time when you felt strong, resourceful and confident. Think of a time when, if you'd have been criticized at that point, you would have been calm about it and taken the positive learning from the situation. Associate into it by imagining yourself there: get the picture, the sounds, everything you heard and felt. Some people find this easier with their eyes closed.

▶ Step 3. When you are really in that moment use your anchor and hold the anchor there while you associate so that the two are connected for you.

▶ Step 4. As the feeling subsides, remove the anchor and break state; this means you need to open your eyes, walk around and give yourself a shake to relax.

▶ Step 5. When you're ready, repeat the exercise. It could be that you want to use another experience and anchor that as well. This is called chaining anchors and can make your anchor even stronger. Use the same anchor then and recall another occasion when you felt strong and resourceful, associating into it as before. Again use the anchor when you're fully 'in it' and remove it once the feeling starts to fade. That way it is only the strongest emotions you are anchoring.

Do this exercise a few times so that when someone criticizes you, all you need to do is apply your anchor to be able to respond appropriately and resourcefully.

....

→ Look for the positive intention

Be curious about the positive intention. When you experience criticism do you immediately become defensive, focusing internally on yourself and what could be at fault in you?

Instead, focus outward and wonder what the person criticizing you wants you to learn. Assuming the critic has a positive intention and wants you to learn from what they are giving you is a resourceful way of handling criticism.

If you have children you will know this very well. We don't criticize our children because we are mean and nasty do we?! No, we want them to learn from their mistakes because we love them and want the best for them. So if this is how we give criticism ourselves why would we not apply this strategy when we ourselves receive criticism?

When someone criticizes you, no matter in what way, be curious and wonder how you can use the criticism in order to do something better in future. What you have been given is feedback, which can be used to learn from.

Exercise 34

Think about the last time someone criticized you or something you had done, whether directly or indirectly. Now imagine you are in their shoes. In their place: what positive intention do you have? Be curious about what it might feel like to be them. What would they like you to learn from this? Write the learning below.

_____

_____

_____

_____

_____

_____

_____

_____

_____

_____

_____

_____

_____

....

FEEL THE FEAR AND DO IT ANYWAY!

Many people fear failure and stay in their comfort zone.
That way everything is easy, doable and there is little risk of
failure or criticism.

It's when you move out of your comfort zone – speak up,
say something controversial or do something unpopular –
that you are more likely to experience criticism. The
problem here is that you are focusing on the negative
instead of giving yourself a 'pat on the back' for doing
something brave. Your belief is that comfort zone = safe
and outside this zone is scary.

Exercise 35

Think of a time when you left your comfort zone and it was perhaps initially scary but then turned out to be very exciting and enjoyable. Maybe you've been on one of those terrifying rides at a theme park, screamed your head off but then enjoyed it so much you went back on it again?! Have you been in a very fast car or skied faster than normal down a very steep slope, been on the back of a motorbike, or done a bungee jump? Whatever it is, write it down here.

_____

_____

_____

_____

_____

_____

_____

Can you appreciate that scary can also be exciting? Actors often say that the physical reactions they get before they go on stage (sweaty palms and palpitations) can be identical to the feeling they get when they are scared or excited and that it can be hard to know which it is.

Fear of failure ensures you stay in your comfort zone and never venture out to avoid being called to account and found lacking. On the other hand if you stay there on 'Easy Street' you will not achieve all you are capable of.

The positive intention of your fear is for you to protect yourself, but ask yourself: could you still protect yourself out of the comfort zone? Of course you could!

There are many ways you can still meet the positive intention of your fear and protect yourself, by:

► changing the belief that you can't handle criticism

► preparing beforehand

► practising until you feel confident

► asking for feedback in order to improve

► using your anchor for confidence

► having a compelling outcome.

How do you change the belief that you can't handle criticism? The best way is to think about times when you handled criticism *well*. Sometimes we're inclined to generalize and tell ourselves that we 'never' handle something well when in fact we have simply deleted those times from our memory and focused on the bad experiences leading to a sense of feeling overwhelmed with negative thoughts.

Another problem can be that someone in the past has said 'you can't take criticism very well can you?' and because you valued that person's opinion you hold it as a truth. Take stock now and think of occasions when this has not been true and recognize that you do have this skill and can use it whenever you need to.

The belief that you cannot take criticism is a 'limiting belief' in that it prevents you taking any chances, putting yourself forward and giving your opinions, so the sooner you replace it with another belief the better!

Exercise 36

Think of a time when you handled criticism well and treated it as feedback you could learn from.

➜ When was it?

_____

_____

_____

_____

➜ Who was there?

_____

_____

_____

_____

➜ What frame of mind were you in?

_____

_____

_____

_____

_____

➜ What was said?

_____

_____

_____

_____

_____

➜ What enabled you to respond resourcefully on that occasion?

_____

_____

_____

_____

_____

You see you do have the skill!

....

If you have low self-esteem, you will see criticism as confirming your poor opinion of yourself. It then becomes a vicious circle and on-going – you're almost watching out for criticism even when it is not intended. The tips above, such as disassociating and looking for the positive intention, will help you with this.

Preparation and practice in many situations will be a good investment for situations which are unfamiliar and which could lead to criticism and a sense of failure. For example, you'd never think of erecting a shed without first reading the instructions and having an image in your head of what it should look like when it's constructed.

Getting into the habit of asking for feedback from colleagues at work, friends and family allows us to constantly monitor what's going well and what needs more work. It is a part of your on-going personal development. The easiest way to do this is to ask, 'Well, what did you think?'

When giving feedback to others use the feedback 'sandwich'. This starts with an overall positive comment, such as 'I liked it'. Then you move on to what you'd have liked to see more of or less of, such as 'I'd have liked a few more charts to illustrate the points you made' or 'I think fewer quotes perhaps'. You then finish upbeat with what was good overall, e.g. 'I think overall, though, it went very well.' If you are in a position to, introduce others to the idea that you'd like your own feedback in this format.

Your anchor for confidence will always be a great asset in feedback situations, so use it!

Finally, always set a compelling outcome. In any situation, have an idea of what you want to get from a discussion, meeting, interaction or review. Once you know what you want and can visualize it, you're almost there. What remains to happen should be done in rapport: feedback should be given and received in rapport and with the positive intention a priority. Rapport is the subject of the next chapter.

→ Focus points

You have learned in this chapter that there are many different forms of feedback:

- ▶ Overt and covert (direct or indirect, to you or about you)
- ▶ Verbal and non-verbal (in verbal language or body language)

Our response to feedback will vary according to:

► Our mood or state

► Our relationship to the person giving the feedback

► The content or subject of the feedback

► The way the feedback is delivered

In order to take control of our response and then reframe it as a learning experience we need to:

► Disassociate

► Hold the belief that the feedback has a positive intention for us

► Be curious about what that positive intention could be

► Take the learning

► Remember the meaning of the communication or behaviour is what is received: not what you intended it to be but what resulted.

What have I learned?

➔ Next time I receive positive feedback what will I do differently?

_____

_____

_____

➔ Next time I receive negative feedback what will I do differently?

_____

_____

_____

➔ How could I help those close to me by using a feedback sandwich?

_____

_____

_____

➔ How could disassociating help me in a feedback situation?

_____

_____

_____

Summary

In this chapter we have discovered that there are different types of feedback; some we manage better than others. We can use techniques such as disassociation and anchoring to manage our response. When we appreciate the positive intention, we get the learning.

Where to next?

Most of us feel more confident and self-assured when we are with people who we know care about us, usually friends and family. But how do we grow our circle of friends and how do we make positive contacts when we meet people for the first time? How we achieve rapport and build on it is the subject of the next chapter.

5 Making and keeping friends

In this chapter you will learn:
- ▶ *How to socialize effectively in rapport*
- ▶ *How to make friends and keep them*
- ▶ *How to communicate so that what is understood is what you intended*

Making new friends, maintaining friendships with old friends and feeling important to others, helps build our self-esteem because we feel that if people like us then we have value. The reverse is also true, and when we struggle to connect socially where we see others thrive, we can feel low self-esteem.

In these situations we are being externally referenced. We are judging ourselves according to the feedback we perceive from other people as opposed to how we actually feel about ourselves. This is perfectly normal but if you tend to focus mostly on how others perceive you, social situations can become a nightmare if you find it difficult to connect with other people.

In this chapter you will learn some good tips for how to connect socially, whether that is in the work context or outside work. Before we go on to explore this in detail. Try to alter your current state. In order to connect socially you need to be in a curious state. You need to want to know more about people and be curious about them ... genuinely curious.

Exercise 37

Think of a time when you were really curious. It could be about anything: a person, a riveting programme on TV or an interesting article in the paper. The point is that the centre of your focus was outside yourself at that time.

Decide on an action that you can associate with this feeling (different from the one you chose for the last anchoring exercise). Now associate into that curious feeling. You need to be thinking 'I wonder why ... what could be happening here...'; maybe you're imagining that you are watching a 'whodunnit' on TV?

As you feel more and more curious, use your anchor and as the curiosity fades, release it (you only want to be anchoring when you're at your most curious).

Repeat this anchoring process a few times so you can use it before an event.

MATCHING AND MISMATCHING

Do you notice that you have lots in common with the people you get on with? Maybe you dress alike, like the same movies, read the same books, eat the same food? We tend to naturally match those we get on with, but what's more we also seek out what we have in common. We notice similarities because we *want* to get on.

When we spot something we don't like or something that is different, we might suggest they're having a bad day, or we dismiss it as out of character. It's possible of course that we too have that same characteristic but don't want to acknowledge it.

When we want to make friends and connect with other people we therefore need to be curious about what we might have in common with the other person we've met. Look for similarities. Look to agree. This is the 'yes ... and...' structure where you add to what they've said while agreeing.

As soon as there is a disagreement conversation jars and stalls. There is a break in the flow and this is often the time the person you are talking to moves away. If that sometimes happens to you at social occasions, ask yourself, 'What did I say or do just before they moved off?'

Watch out for the word 'but' as it signals disagreement, and, despite being only three letters long, fights above its weight. People can't help noticing the 'but' and if they were only half-listening before will prick up their ears and pay attention to what you say after the 'but'. So even if you were agreeing before, what you say now will appear to mismatch. For example 'I really agree with you, but don't you think...' is mismatching and rapport is now lost.

VISUAL, AUDITORY AND KINAESTHETIC (VAK)

We each have a preferred style of communicating depending on how we process our world. These styles are called 'visual', 'auditory' and 'kinaesthetic'. You may already know which you are.

If you think in pictures and notice what you see rather than what you hear or feel then you are visual. A visual person will pay a lot of attention to their physical surroundings, making them as attractive and pleasing to the eye as possible.

They will spend time on their appearance and notice yours. Design and colours will matter to them in what they buy. They may well be quite arty and have hobbies like photography or drawing, painting, sewing, designing and so on. Visual people speak quickly as they turn images into words and frequently look up when they speak, to the left to recall an image or to the right to construct one.

When you want to build rapport with a visual person, match the type of words they use, which will be words like: 'see', 'look', 'view', e.g. 'Do you see what I'm saying?', 'Do you like the look of that?' or 'What's your view?'

If you notice what you hear and enjoy a good chat rather than watching a film, then you could well be auditory. Auditory people tend to talk slower than visual people, taking care to choose words precisely to reflect what they mean to say. They listen to what you have to say too, paying attention to the words you use.

An auditory person may pick you up on a word because they really want to understand you and want to know which word you mean so they can stay in rapport. They get easily distracted by someone talking loudly across the room or noises around them because they hear what non-auditory people barely notice. They may well be musical and enjoy listening to music and playing an instrument. They probably enjoy listening to the radio and prefer having something particular to listen to, or even complete silence, to noises from other people around them.

When you want to build rapport with an auditory person give them time to say what they want to say and speak slowly (at their speed) when responding. They will prefer to discuss face to face or over the phone rather than by text or email. Match their words, which will be 'hear', 'listen', 'sounds', e.g. 'Do you hear what I'm saying?'; 'Listen to him!' and 'That sounds great.'

If you are quite active and physical you may well be kinaesthetic although, of course, plenty of visual and auditory people are sporty and enjoy exercise! Kinaesthetic people will tend to be fidgety and not enjoy sitting still very much. They notice the temperature of their physical environment and will want to have control over it, not wanting to be in a room that is stuffy or too warm. Kinaesthetic people prefer hands-on meetings, such as workshops, rather than being talked to (which an auditory person would enjoy) or being given a PowerPoint presentation (more appealing to visual people).

When you want to build rapport with a kinaesthetic person, keep the conversation active and involving for them. Ask them to do something and maybe keep active while you're talking: try walking and talking or having a drink or a coffee, or a game of golf. They like to be active so you'll get the best from them if you are too. They'll use action words like 'get', 'hold', and 'grasp', e.g. 'Do you get what I mean?', 'Hold on to that thought' and 'I don't think you've grasped my meaning'.

You might use any or all of these styles of communicating during the course of any day, but there will be one that you'll revert to more often and feel more comfortable with. Which is it? Which of these descriptions best fits with you?

Exercise 38

Having read about VAK, now divide up your friends and work colleagues, family and others you socialize with according to whether they are visual, auditory or kinaesthetic.

Visual	Auditory	Kinaesthetic

(Continued)

Visual	Auditory	Kinaesthetic

What do you notice? Do you see any patterns? Are there more names in one category than another? Where are YOU? If you're not sure where someone belongs, put them in all the categories for the moment. Then, as you work through the exercise, it will become clear where they belong.

You may be wondering what on earth this has to do with self-esteem! Well it has everything to do with it. If you can judge the VAK of the person you're talking to, and those you live with and work with, you will achieve good rapport with them. This leads to better relationships and in turn it leads to a higher sense of self-worth which is self-esteem. How much better we feel about ourselves when we can experience a sense of rapport; it gives us the feeling that someone likes us and wants to spend time in our company.

→ Meta-programmes

There's more we can do to ensure we get on with people and this is using what we call meta-programmes in NLP. They are in the form of a scale where we label each end. You've already met one of them – 'match/mismatch'. Here are the others:

▶ towards/away from

▶ internal/external

▶ choices/process

- big chunk/small chunk
- past/present/future
- associated/disassociated

The last one (**associated/disassociated**) you have also met in the context of anchoring. When we anchor we associate into a feeling, situation or experience. That means we live it as if it were happening right now and we bring on all the feelings attached to it. When we are associated in a social context we make a strong connection with the person we are talking with and really feel what they feel and take on their emotions as if they were our own.

This is obviously appropriate in some contexts but probably not at work where we need to be somewhat more disassociated and less emotionally involved (depending on the work we do of course). How do we put ourselves in such a state, you may ask?

Remember how you put yourself into the associated state for anchoring? You closed your eyes and remembered everything about the situation or experience you wanted to anchor as if it was happening now. When we want or need to disassociate it may also help to close your eyes (at least while you practise).

Imagine you could fly above your body and look down on the scene and what is happening now. Imagine a sort of 'out of body' experience. From where you now see the situation you should be able to see all parties in the conversation, and can equally observe you and the other people in a way that is detached, impartial and unemotional.

The disassociated state is a good one for accepting feedback if you have a tendency to low self-esteem because it gives you a certain amount of emotional protection. This is therefore an excellent state to have available for confrontations with teenagers! Use the disassociated state when you feel vulnerable or feel low self-esteem because in this state you will be able to get a more two-sided view.

Exercise 39

There is a great NLP exercise we can do using this meta-programme. It is called Perceptual Positioning and we use it to enable us to see things from a different point of view. When you are experiencing low self-esteem, instead of becoming ever more associated into it with the risk of becoming depressed, do this exercise in order to see things afresh.

▶ Step 1. Set out three chairs or cushions in a triangle.

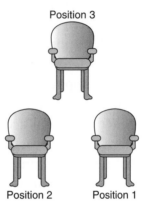

Position 3

Position 2   Position 1

▶ Step 2. Position 1 is YOU. Start there. Think about how you are feeling about your confidence right now.

▶ Step 3. Do you sometimes have an inner voice that tells you that you are useless? This is Position 2 so go and sit in Position 2 and be that voice, that critical inner voice. Associate into it and really take on the persona of the inner voice.

▶ Step 4. Now go back to Position 1 and respond as you again to what you've heard from Position 2. You may want to stand up for yourself and counter what you said as Position 2. This exercise involves switching between Position 1 and Position 2 allowing you and your inner critic or judge to talk to each other.

▶ Step 5. When you have said all you have to say at each position; go and sit at Position 3 where you disassociate and imagine you are an impartial observer of the discussion that just took place. In Position 3 what did you observe, what did you hear, how did you feel? What do you have to say to each position? What learning can you offer them?

▶ Step 6. When you have said what you have to say from Position 3 you can then respond from Position 1 and say what you plan to do, and how you will think and feel differently now.

··

Notice in others whether they are associated or disassociated and match them to achieve rapport. When you want to build rapport with someone who is very associated it can feel rather intense, possibly even uncomfortable, but to build rapport you need to go with the flow, match the state and step into their shoes (not literally of course!). If on the other hand you need to build rapport with someone who is disassociated, then you would again match their preference to step back from the situation and view it dispassionately yourself, as if it was happening to someone else.

TOWARDS/AWAY FROM

Towards/away from is the next meta-programme we will look at. Some people focus on what they do want and that is 'towards'; for example they think about the positive things they want to achieve in life such as work success, a good marriage, health, happiness, being fit and so on. Others focus on what they don't want, which is 'away from', such as poor health, debt, unemployment or divorce.

There is no right or wrong way to be; just be aware of how you think at the moment and be curious as to whether by focusing on another way, you may get a different result in terms of your self-esteem. Also, notice how confident people think and behave. In general, when you focus on what you want, you get it.

Exercise 40

Let's take health as an example. Read the following questions and circle the answer most applicable to you: a, b or c.

1 **Do you take vitamin supplements in order to be healthy or to avoid ill health?**

   a To be healthy

   b To avoid ill health

   c I don't take them

2 **Do you eat healthy foods to stay healthy or avoid illness or obesity?**

   a To stay healthy

   b To avoid illness or obesity

   c I don't eat healthy foods

3 **Do you exercise to be fit or to avoid getting overweight?**

   a To be fit

   b To avoid getting overweight

   c I don't exercise

4 **Do you stretch after exercise to keep your muscles flexible or to avoid them getting stiff?**

   a To keep flexible

   b To avoid getting stiff

   c I don't stretch

5 Do you take antibiotics to get better or to avoid getting worse?

   a To get better

   b To avoid getting worse

   c I don't take antibiotics

It's clear I'm sure as you answer these questions how you process and whether you are 'towards' (answer a) or 'away from' (answer b). Just think though, if you changed this and switched to focus on what you want instead of what you don't want, how it might make a difference in your life. If you answered 'c' maybe you need to love your body more?!

....

Weight loss is clearly an 'away from' orientation and focuses on what you are losing rather than what you gain. People on diets talk about what they can't eat, have given up and what they want to lose. When do we normally feel pleased to have lost something; it goes against the grain doesn't it? If you want to have a trimmer figure focus on what you *do* want and notice the difference in results.

Aim for a particular weight or size and establish it as a compelling outcome, something you really want and will commit to working towards. The problem is also that the more you focus on what you can't have, the more it becomes important. The one thing dieters think about is eating, the very thing they need to do less of!

Debt is another one. Do you want to avoid getting into debt or do you focus on keeping to a budget? Thinking about what you can't afford and what you haven't got in the bank is not a healthy way to manage money. Instead, work out what you have got and enjoy the achievement of keeping within it.

Generally, what we focus on is what we get so the more you focus on what you want (a 'towards' meta-programme) the more likely you will be to achieve it. Therefore, in the context of self-esteem, instead of worrying about social situations, standing up in front of your colleagues or asking someone out on a date, focus on what you do want. Visualize yourself being confident (if you are visual), imagine what people will say (if you are auditory) and imagine how you will feel and what will happen (if you are kinaesthetic) and you are practically there!

When you want to build rapport with someone who is 'towards', follow their language pattern and talk about what you *do* want and match them. If they are 'away from', again, copy their pattern and talk about what you want to avoid. When you need them to do something that is 'towards', you will need to mismatch but in rapport, i.e. 'I know you want to avoid a confrontation, and we don't want to upset the client as we can't afford to lose the business, so what *can* we do to keep him sweet?'

INTERNAL/EXTERNAL

Do you rely on other people's approval or do you know yourself if you have done a good job? If you look for other people's approval and focus more on them, then you are 'externally referenced', whereas if you make your own decisions about your performance based on your own values and expectations then you are 'internally referenced'.

We call this the **internal/external** meta-programme. In a nutshell it is about how much the opinion of others matters to you. Of course it will vary for you depending on which people you are thinking about, because it may matter a lot what your boss and your partner think of you, but matter less what the checkout assistant at your local supermarket thinks. So where are you along the scale?

The scale below equates to how much other people's reactions, feedback or opinions matter to you. It runs from 1—10, with 1 being 'does not matter at all what they think of me' and 10 meaning that these people's opinions would greatly affect what you say and do.

Matters very much

10

9

8

7

6

5

4

3

2

Does not matter

1

Along the scale write down the names or types of people whom you would place at each score point. There may also be a difference depending on the topic. For example, you may mind more what your partner thinks about your weight than what your mum thinks, and you may be more externally referenced about your game of tennis than your golf because in tennis you are perhaps playing with a partner and don't want to let them down, but in golf you are playing as an individual.

→ What did you notice while doing this exercise? Write it down.

_____

_____

_____

_____

_____

_____

_____

_____

The reason we need to understand this is so we can use it to alter our self-esteem. As long as we compare ourselves unfavourably with others, look for their approval and care what they think of us, we lose control because we can't control what or how they think or how they respond. When we check in with ourselves, our own values and beliefs, then we can make our own judgement about how well we are doing.

Do you find yourself shrugging off compliments when someone praises you for a good golf shot or a good meeting, a well-presented room or something similar, because you know you could have done it better? Well in that situation you are being internally referenced – you are not taking their word for it, you have your own standards and believe you've fallen short. If you are completely unable to decide whether what you've done is good until a few people say it is, then you're being externally referenced and will find it much harder to improve your self-esteem because you're reliant on factors outside of your control.

So what do you do about it if you are externally referenced? You start deciding for yourself what is good and what isn't and give yourself credit for knowing which is which.

When you want to build rapport with someone who is externally referenced, you need to acknowledge that other people matter to them so you'd refer to them in your conversation by asking what 'X' thinks of their plan or whether 'X' agrees. When you want to build rapport with someone who is internally referenced you need to ask them what they think about the topic.

CHOICES/PROCESS

Do you like to spend time considering your options or do you like to just press on and get things done? Are you a 'choices' or 'process' driven person?

When I go out with my brother to a restaurant we both look at the menu, of course, but what happens next is very different. I peruse the options, make a decision and close the menu ready to start our chatter. He strokes his chin slowly, goes back and forth through the pages and mutters 'shall I have this, or this, or maybe that'. You've guessed it! I am process and he is choices. In fact we are pretty much at opposite ends of this scale as I hate choices and he adores them. However, in a different situation, when we went on holiday together to Barcelona, it was me who was enjoying the choices of what we could visit and he had a very regimented plan because he'd previously spent hours deliberating his choices so that he could make the best use of his time.

As you can imagine, in most situations it's good to be able to slide up and down this scale because in a business context we often need to consider options before embarking on any plan of action. Then there are other situations when getting on with the plan is the only way to get things done and considering options is simply a delaying tactic. Having a mix of choices and process people on your team is a good solution to this. This would also be true of marriage where, if both partners were keen on options, no decisions would ever be made!

When you want to build rapport with someone who likes choices, it is a mistake to give them just one option; instead offer them a number of options, any of which would suit you. If you want to build rapport with a process person, they simply want to know what needs to be done; they need a list of jobs or tasks and then they will get on with it. Do not confuse them by offering them options because this will cause them to lose motivation for the overall task and it will certainly break rapport.

BIG CHUNK/SMALL CHUNK

The next one always reminds me of chocolate! It is called **big chunk/small chunk**.

Big chunk people tend to think in broad brush terms, concepts rather than detail. Do you love to get embroiled in detail, planning holidays, outings, campaigns and so on, or do you prefer to 'take a stab at it', and just get the general idea?

Case study

When I'm cooking I just take a glance at the ingredients in the recipe and assume I can substitute pretty much any of them with whatever I have in my fridge. I don't measure anything, I guess the quantities and I don't time anything I cook, I simply check on it occasionally. My husband, on the other hand, is extremely precise and follows a recipe to the letter, measures everything within an inch of its life and checks his watch to time each stage of the process. His cooking is much better than mine but mine isn't inedible. He is small chunk and focuses on the detail whereas I am big chunk and focus on the end result in a general way.

As with the other meta-programmes, there is no right and wrong and, again, this is a sliding scale where you might be into the detail in one part of your life but more prepared to relax it in others.

Case study

My friend Jane has recently bought an old cottage which she is renovating. She has been overwhelmed by the process which has now dragged on for nearly a year as she had to have so much done and couldn't afford to have it all done in one go. She had a clear vision for the cottage but she has found the minutiae particularly overwhelming: all

---

the detail she needs to address in each room and for each part of the project. The only way she could avoid being swamped by it was to write 'to do lists' and tick each thing off as it was done. Now Jane has never been a 'list' person, so this was a whole new experience, but she had to take control of the process before it took control of her!

When you want to build rapport with a small chunk person, give them detail and precision because they will be overwhelmed by the enormity of a whole concept. Equally, when building rapport with a big chunker avoid detail and give them the big picture, letting them work out what detail they need, if any.

In work you need both types of thinking in your team don't you? It might be fun to experiment in your non-work life how it feels to slide up and down the scale.

Exercise 42

If you sense that you are usually big chunk, take something you do regularly and break it into the detail. So, for example, for your morning routine, instead of thinking 'I just get ready for work' list all the detail.

→ Decide on the task and write it here:

_____

_____

_____

_____

Now break it down into detailed steps.

1 _____

2 _____

3 _____

4 _____

5 _____

6 _____

7 _____

8 _____

9 _____

10 _____

If you're usually like this and would like to experiment with what it feels like to be big chunk, try this out.

Think of something you do regularly and write all the stages below.

→ The task or activity is:

_____

_____

_____

_____

_____

_____

1 _____

2 _____

3 _____

4 _____

5 _____

6 _____

7 _____

8 _____

9 _____

10 _____

Now collect the steps above together and write down here what you do as ONE task:

_____

_____

_____

_____

_____

_____

Remember, when you want to build rapport with someone who is big chunk you need to avoid detail and look at the bigger picture: what does what you are saying actually mean? Conversely, if you want to build rapport with someone who is small chunk you need to give them detail and lots of it. If they ask you how to do something they want instructions.

....

PAST/PRESENT/FUTURE

The last meta-programme we will look at here is **past/ present/future**. This is about where we place our emphasis. Do you tend to refer back to things that happened in the past, the last time you did that thing, or do you think about what you have to do later, where you need to be and what needs to be done for some future event? In business we are often thinking more than a year ahead, in terms of product launches, new product development and so on.

> **Case study**
>
> My piano teacher teaches music in a local school and is, therefore, also in charge of all the concerts. She has to start thinking about the next concert months in advance so she has the children properly rehearsed. She is always focused on the future. She thinks ahead, plans, saves for holidays and trips, plans fundraising events and is always on Facebook telling us what she has to do that day, and where she will be going. She is future orientated of course.

Lots of people like to refer back to their experiences of the past because they want to avoid making the same mistakes ('away from' thinking) or want to learn from what they did before to make the result even better next time ('towards' thinking).

For a healthy and happy lifestyle many people believe one should live in the present in order to have 'time to smell the roses', but this isn't usually possible if you're juggling jobs, home and children.

Exercise 43

It pays to be curious though and to be prepared to move up and down this continuum. Let's think about something you have to do next month. What is it?

_____

_____

_____

_____

Now remember the last time you did something very similar to this. How did it go?

_____

_____

_____

_____

Give yourself some feedback. What went well and what could have been better?

➜ What went well?

_____

_____

_____

_____

_____

→What could have been better?

_____

_____

_____

_____

_____

→How will you change what you did for the next time?

_____

_____

_____

_____

_____

If you usually focus on what happened in the past, maybe previous experiments or the last time you gave this lesson or talk, move into the present and be in the moment, experiencing everything that is happening right now.

If you usually live in the present, take a moment to think ahead to what you will be doing tomorrow or next week, and make an arrangement or a plan for a few weeks ahead.

Now record what you found when you time travelled.

_____

_____

_____

_____

_____

When you want to build rapport with someone who emphasizes a different time from you, the best way to get on is to join them where they are.

....

The meta-programmes are sliding scales which you will find yourself moving along and being in a different place at different times and occasions in your life. However, you will find that your natural tendency is to be at one end or the other and in order to have rapport, make friends and build self-esteem you will need to be flexible, make different choices of how to communicate using their preference, their meta-programme.

We can do this at all levels, not only in conversation. By matching body language we can also connect and build rapport. This will be covered in the next chapter.

→ Focus points

Our self-esteem can be raised by improving the way we connect with those around us. Increased rapport produces positive feedback and high self-esteem. Tips for achieving good rapport are:

► Be curious.

► Notice similarities – what you have in common.

► Seek to agree – 'yes... and...'.

► Match their meta-programme.

► Match their time.

What have I learned?

→ Which is my preference – visual, auditory or kinaesthetic?

_____

_____

_____

→ When I am in rapport with someone what do I notice about my physiology?

_____

_____

_____

→ How would I go about achieving rapport with someone who has a different preference to me?

_____

_____

_____

→ Now that I know the meta-programmes how will I communicate differently with my partner/child?

_____

_____

_____

Summary

When we feel that people like us, and that we have friends, it builds our self esteem because it confirms that we have value or worth. By matching the VAK (visual, auditory and kinaesthetic) preferences and the meta-programmes of those we connect with, we achieve good rapport. In order to step into their shoes we can do a perceptual positioning exercise.

Where to next?

Whether we like it or not, we judge people before they have even opened their mouth. Most communication is non-verbal. In the seconds before we start a conversation we have already decided whether we like a person and the rapport building has already begun. What we wear, how we present ourselves, the choices we make about how we look, walk and behave all affect how we communicate and the communication we receive from others is also based on these factors. In the next chapter we will explore how this works.

6 Body language

In this chapter you will learn:
- ▶ *How people make assumptions about you based on how you look, which are in turn based on their values and beliefs. You are doing this too.*
- ▶ *How to use a Circle of Excellence to achieve a confident and resourceful physiology*
- ▶ *Helpful general pointers on rapport-building body language*

People make assumptions about you before you start to speak. They learn about you from how you look, how you stand or sit and your eye contact and facial expressions. The first interaction you make is non-verbal. In this chapter you will learn how to make the best first impression with your body language and how to give yourself confidence just by altering your body posture.

How often have you made an assumption about someone at a distance without knowing them or speaking to them? On what basis are we making these judgements?

Exercise 44

Here are a few images of people who you don't know. In the box alongside each one write down what you think they'd be like, whether you'd like to befriend them and what it is about them that draws you to them.

© tale/Shutterstock

© Elena Elisseeva/Shutterstock

© NotarYES/Shutterstock

© Felix Mizioznikov/Shutterstock

What were you focusing on? Tick the ones that apply.

→ Facial expression ☐

→ The pose itself ☐

→ The hands ☐

→ Clothing ☐

→ Age ☐

→ Gender ☐

→ What they are doing ☐

Now think about how you present yourself. Have a look in a mirror.

→ What do your clothes say about you?

_____

_____

_____

_____

_____

➜ What does your facial expression suggest to others?

_____

_____

_____

_____

➜ What does your age or perceived age indicate to someone who doesn't know you?

_____

_____

_____

_____

➜ How do you use your hands and arms?

_____

_____

_____

_____

➜ What is your usual pose when you meet someone?

_____

_____

_____

_____

_____

We look different when we have high self-esteem. Play around with your physiology and be curious about how your thinking affects what you convey to others. Here are a few emotions to experiment with. Underneath each, note what can be observed by others.

➜ Confident

_____

➜ Interested

_____

➜ Thoughtful

_____

➜ Sad

_____

➜ Angry

_____

➜ Impatient

_____

➜ Loving

_____

→Tired

_____

→Happy

_____

→Busy

_____

→Shy

_____

→Embarrassed

_____

→Scared

_____

→Disgusted

_____

Were some of the emotions harder than others? Which ones?

_____

Which resulted in similar physiology?

_____

Which could have been confusing for others to determine?

_____

Let's focus on the confident physiology as we're working on self-esteem. How do you look when you're feeling super confident? We're going to do an exercise now called the 'Circle of Excellence' whereby you create an imaginary circle which you can use whenever you need that confident feeling.

Exercise 45

Draw an imaginary circle on the floor in front of you. It needs to be big enough to stand in comfortably.

▶ Step 1. Think of a time when you felt really confident or when your self-esteem was high. If you are visual then get the image clearly in your head with whatever you can see in the picture. Make the colours and image bright. If you are auditory then recall in your head everything you said and what others said at that time. If you are kinaesthetic, remember what you did and what others were doing. Recall all the feelings you had at that moment.

▶ Step 2. When all the pictures, sounds and actions are strong step into the circle.

▶ Step 3. As they fade, step out.

▶ Step 4. Repeat steps 1–3 until you can access that confident feeling really easily. We need to do this again several times so that our Circle of Excellence contains a number of memories of times when we felt confident and had high self-esteem.

This is very similar to anchoring, but we are using the stepping motion and the sense of being in a circle as our anchor.

PHYSIOLOGY

As you repeat the exercise using other experiences to build a strong anchor in your circle, be aware of your physiology. How are you standing, where are your shoulders and your arms, and where are you looking? This physiology is a part of your anchor and Circle of Excellence. When you want to feel confident, simply recreate that body posture and you'll get the accompanying feelings of high self-esteem.

We communicate so much non-verbally, and impressions about us are formed before we speak, so in order to do a quick physical check on what we are communicating, get into the habit of disassociating. Mentally step out of your own body and imagine someone is looking at you. What do you think they would notice? If it isn't what you want then change your physiology so that it matches what you want to convey.

Here are some general pointers although, for the most part, matching the other person's physiology is a good way to achieve rapport which in turn will give you high self-esteem.

1 Legs and arms need to be uncrossed. Crossed legs or arms give the impression of being defensive.

2 Eye contact should be easy without staring, which will seem rude or intimidating. This also ensures that your head is up and shows you are engaged in the conversation.

3 Own your space by standing or sitting in a way that shows that you are happy to be there rather than wishing you weren't. Legs slightly apart suggest you own the space. Be careful not to invade the other person's space.

4 Shrug your shoulders to check they are relaxed and not hunched up.

5 Occasionally nod while the other person is talking to indicate that you are listening.

6 Keep hands away from your face and avoid fidgeting as it is distracting, although it's fine to use your hands to demonstrate a point.

7 Sit or stand upright without slouching, leaning forward or leaning back.

8 Put down anything you're holding, especially if you have it in front of your neck, bellybutton or groin area as these are so-called 'power zones' and covering any of them is a sign that you feel insecure.

9 Talk slowly and clearly and walk purposefully. Someone rushing about looks out of control.

10 Lastly, be curious and relax; enjoy the connection you're making.

The best way to look confident is to be confident. Remember, actions speak louder than words. Perhaps you'd be surprised to know that 93 per cent of communication is non-verbal.

You can use body language in meetings to demonstrate confidence by sitting close to whoever is running the meeting, and avoiding sitting opposite anyone with whom you tend to disagree or don't get on with, as this can appear confrontational. In addition to applying the ten points above, don't fiddle with papers or your phone.

DRESS

Another aspect of body language is the clothes you wear. What do your clothes say about you? Do they ooze high self-esteem?

How we dress tells people who we are and how we want to be treated. If you want to appear confident, then choose clothes that are smart, professional and show a hint of individuality. You should feel good about what you're wearing and know that it is appropriate for the occasion, whether it's business or social.

Be aware of the culture of the organization you work for or are visiting, or the group you are socializing with. Match your style with the cultural environment so that you don't stand out as being naïve. Know your own style and work with it; wear colours that suit you. Before you leave the house check in the mirror and disassociate. What will others think of you when they see what you are wearing? Is that what you want them to think? Here are the key points to consider when choosing clothes. Make sure they...

▶ suit your personality

▶ are appropriate

▶ are in colours that flatter

▶ are current

▶ are a flattering style that fits well

Exercise 46

How well do you know what suits you?

Think about what you feel most confident wearing for work. Describe it in the space below. Think about the specific outfit, colour, style, fit, accessories and so on.

_____

_____

_____

_____

_____

What about when you're out with friends? What do you wear to feel confident?

_____

_____

_____

_____

_____

Be aware of how clothes make you feel, and choose clothes that will give you that 'feel good' factor for important meetings at work or job interviews. This is also important when you are going out on a first date. Think about what you want to convey about yourself. The first thing the date will notice is what you are wearing, so make sure their first impression is accurate.

· ·

In order to increase your awareness of how clothes affect people's perception of you, start noticing how other people dress and how their choices influence how you behave towards them.

Just as busy hand movements or fiddling with things can distract attention from what you are saying, busy or inappropriate clothes can also distract. If you want to be taken seriously and have your views considered, it is important to dress with this in mind. Fussy jewellery, too much make-up and sexy clothing, while fun in the social environment, can give the impression that you don't belong in the more serious business world (unless perhaps you work in a creative environment).

Your body itself creates an impression. It would be hard to have high self-esteem if people are moving away from you because of bad breath, body odour or very strong perfume or after-shave. You want people to feel comfortable around you.

It's hard to feel confident and have high self-esteem when you feel overweight and sluggish. You can mask this with clever choices of clothing but a long-term solution would be to increase your exercise regime and eat more healthy foods. There are plenty of books around on how to exercise efficiently and what to eat to be healthy. You will feel much more confident when you are happy with how you look, so invest time in this by exercising regularly and making different meal choices.

In a similar vein, hair, face and skin are noticed on first meeting someone so what do yours say about you?

▶ Is your hair well cut and tidy?

▶ Are your nails clean?

▶ Is your make-up appropriate for the occasion?

▶ Are your teeth clean?

This may all seem rather basic and it is. Nevertheless it needs to be spelt out. How you look really does affect how you are judged and how people will respond to you. This in turn affects how you feel about yourself. Therefore, if you have low self-esteem sometimes, think about what you could do to make people's first impression the one you want it to be so that you feel good about yourself.

Exercise 47

Think about the last time someone gave you a compliment about what you were wearing or how you looked. What were you wearing on that occasion and what was there about how you looked that made the difference?

_____

_____

_____

_____

_____

→ Focus points

► Assumptions are made about you and by you based on what you are wearing, how you look, sit or stand, your facial expression and eye contact. What are you communicating? How can you become more aware of this so that you consciously communicate self-esteem?

► When you dress in the morning or before an event where you want to impress people around you, consider these factors:

▷ Do your clothes fit you?

▷ Do the colours suit you?

▷ Are your clothes appropriate for the occasion?

▷ Are they up to date?

▷ Are your shoes clean and unscuffed?

▷ Are your clothes clean and in good condition?

▷ Does the style flatter you?

- Did you know that you wear 20 per cent of the clothes in your wardrobe 80 per cent of the time? Is now a good time to get rid of those you won't wear again and buy some that you will? Think about the occasion you are buying for next time you shop for clothes.

- Test out your facial expressions and body postures using a mirror and ask yourself what you are communicating. Play around to get the best look for the occasion.

- Personal cleanliness is important. Smell is one of the key things people notice and remember. Brush your teeth before meeting people, check for body odour and top up the deodorant if necessary, check for foot odour if you have a tendency to sweat. Get a good haircut and keep body hair out of sight.

What have I learned?

→ What does what I am wearing today tell people about me?

_____

_____

_____

→ Is this my intended message?

_____

_____

_____

→ How would someone know that I liked them; how would it show on my face and in my body language?

_____

_____

_____

→ What three changes to my body language could I make right now to improve my self-esteem?

_____

_____

_____

Summary

People have already decided whether they like us before we've started speaking, so we need to ensure that how we look, and how we stand or sit, conveys the desired impression of who we are. You can mange this by becoming aware of how your feelings are reflected in your body so you can control what you convey. Similarly the clothes you wear tell a story about you. Manage the story so it accords with your values and beliefs; 97% of how you communicate is non-verbal so this is an important aspect to master.

Where to next?

In the next chapter you will learn how to control your state or mood. Perhaps you are easily affected by other people's behaviour or mood? Well, you will learn how to anchor resourceful states and set compelling outcomes for what you want from your interactions.

7 staying positive

In this chapter you will learn:
▶ *How to reframe negative experiences*
▶ *How to manage your state (mood)*
▶ *How to set compelling outcomes and 'towards' goals to stay focused*

It would be too simplistic to say that being confident is all about positive thinking, but the ability to take responsibility for our thinking and subsequent behaviour gives us control over our state and the opportunity to choose how we respond to outside stimuli. Firstly, we have to accept that no-one can make us feel or think in a particular way; we do that ourselves. You know how people say things like...

Just think how hard it would be to actually *make* someone feel something they didn't already feel. The idea that someone can make you feel something you don't already feel is a distortion. Think about the last time you blamed someone for making you feel something bad: when was this? Write it in the space below.

_____

_____

_____

_____

_____

_____

Now think about how they did this. What did they say or do that prompted these emotions?

_____

_____

_____

_____

_____

_____

At some point you decided how you felt and it may not even have been related to what was said. When we feel a certain way we can sometimes misconstrue what is said to us, twist it and form it into something that fits with how we are feeling at the time.

In relationships this happens a lot, doesn't it? Here's a classic:

The only possible answer is 'no', isn't it?

The same is true, of course, of positive feelings such as:

Think about the last time you felt that someone had 'made you feel' something positive. What happened?

- ▶ They smiled at me. ☐
- ▶ They made me laugh. ☐
- ▶ They touched me. ☐
- ▶ They hugged me. ☐
- ▶ They agreed with what I was saying. ☐
- ▶ I made them laugh. ☐
- ▶ They complimented me on what I was wearing. ☐
- ▶ They noticed I'd changed my hair style. ☐
- ▶ They liked my perfume. ☐
- ▶ They liked my work. ☐
- ▶ Something else _____

How exactly did they *make* you feel like that?

_____

_____

_____

_____

_____

_____

_____

You choose how you feel. Consider these comments and think of two different ways of interpreting each one.

a) Making the assumption that the comment was positive.

b) Making the assumption negative.

I haven't seen you around for ages.

a) _____

b) _____

Where did you get that dress/suit?

a) _____

b) _____

I wish I had as much time as you do for sport.

a) _____

b) _____

In an unfamiliar situation, or with people you don't know and don't trust yet, it can be a dilemma. What do they mean? Is the comment meant seriously or is it just their sense of humour? Are they being sarcastic or ironic? Do I smile or take offence? A whole raft of conflicting emotions will emerge and you need to stop and consider how to respond.

Here's how the thought process might go:

If I said _____ I would mean

_____

▶ If someone else overheard this how would they interpret it?

_____

▶ What would be the most positive way of interpreting it?

_____

▶ Is this the most appropriate response in this situation?

_____

▶ What choice will I make?

_____

This thought process happens in seconds, especially when you are in a new situation because your mind is running on fast speed. There are ways you can give yourself longer to think about your response and ways you can verify what the speaker meant if you are unsure. The best and quickest way is to just repeat back to them the last few words, or a few key words, emphasizing the one you're not sure about, with an upward inflection like this:

Q. That's a pretty unusual serve you've got there!

A. An *unusual* serve?

This enables the speaker to explain what they meant and it will then become clearer how you should respond. You stay in rapport, whereas if you'd said 'What do you mean, unusual?' this would have sounded slightly confrontational. Another way we can find out more is by adopting a questioning stance.

The key to unfamiliar situations becoming manageable and capable of building rather than destroying your self-esteem is to establish a compelling outcome in advance. Remember, a compelling outcome is a goal or objective that just belongs in that single situation and reflects what you want to achieve from it. Make sure that your compelling outcome is 'towards', what you want to achieve rather than 'away from'. An 'away from' goal would be 'I hope I don't go to pieces in there' or 'I just want to get out of there without any awkward questions that I can't answer'. Think about an unfamiliar situation you have ahead of you – write about it below.

_____

_____

_____

_____

_____

_____

_____

_____

_____

_____

Now write down a few possible goals or compelling outcomes you could have about this situation.

1 _____

_____

_____

2 _____

_____

_____

3 _____

_____

_____

4 _____

_____

_____

5 _____

_____

_____

Are your goals 'towards' and phrased in the positive?

Are they things that you can control yourself? It's all very well setting goals but you can only control your own behaviour. For example, if your goal is to make a sale, you can't control the other suppliers putting in lower prices or bids for the work, nor can you control your client's budget; therefore you won't be able to ensure a sale regardless of what you do or how much you want it.

We also can't control other people's feelings, so avoid setting outcomes such as 'I want her to feel happy/proud/excited' and so on. Your compelling outcome needs to factor in behaviour that you can control. The other person's feelings will be influenced by other considerations beyond your control such as mood, tiredness, other people's input and so on.

The goals also need to be quite specific and therefore measurable. A compelling outcome in a negotiation might be to get a better discount for your company but how much discount would satisfy you as being 'better'? Set a specific percentage or a range that will be acceptable. How can you stay positive if you don't know whether you've done well and should be congratulated on your success?

Exercise 48

Here are some situations you might encounter; have a go at suggesting a compelling outcome for each one. Remember to make it positive, 'towards' and something you can control.

→ A discussion with your teenage daughter about what time she's to be picked up from a party.

_____

_____

_____

_____

→ A meeting with your boss about next year's sales forecast.

_____

_____

_____

_____

→A chat with a friend about sharing the school run.

_____

_____

_____

_____

→A talk with your neighbour about his son's music being played loud late at night.

_____

_____

_____

_____

→A chat with your partner about cutting down on their spending.

_____

_____

_____

_____

→A call to the bank about them charging you for an unauthorized overdraft.

_____

_____

_____

_____

→A call to the council about some fly-tipping up your road.

_____

_____

_____

_____

→A chat with your neighbour about their dog barking during the day.

_____

_____

_____

_____

→Your six-monthly review at work.

_____

_____

_____

_____

→A discussion with your child-minder about her increase in fees.

_____

_____

_____

_____

How could you go about meeting these outcomes? What could you do? This might involve research, preparation or practice. Visualizing yourself after you have achieved the outcome is another sure fire way of achieving it. After all, if you can't even imagine what it would be like and feel like to successfully achieve your outcome, what chance do you have?

....

We all experience negative situations from time to time and the ability to reframe them is a great asset for both our own self-esteem and that of others we care about or are responsible for. Here is the six-step reframe exercise. Reframing is looking at something in a different and positive way that initially appears negative or unhelpful.

Exercise 49

Let's first consider some situations that you might wish to reframe. Write down below three situations that you have either experienced recently or are currently experiencing which you would like to reframe in a positive way.

1 _____

_____

_____

_____

2 _____

_____

_____

_____

3 _____

_____

_____

_____

Now here is the six-step reframe.

▶ Step 1. Decide which of these situations you want to work on for this exercise.

▶ Step 2. Ask this negative part of you whether it is willing to communicate with you. Perhaps it is something you have ignored in the past, pretended wasn't anything to do with you, decided wasn't important or wasn't your fault. You are now bringing it to your consciousness and need to check that this is OK.

▶ Step 3. Find the positive intention. Having established communication with this negative experience we need to assume that it has a good intention for you, so what is it? Be curious and creative. There is some learning in this negative experience, we just need to look for it.

▶ Step 4. Now be creative and come up with three alternative ways to achieve that positive intention.

▶ Step 5. Evaluate these options. How acceptable are they? How are they better (or are they?) than what you actually do or did? If they aren't you'll have to go back a step and come up with some more options. Keep going until you have one that you are willing to have a go at.

▶ Step 6. Finally check that the chosen option for trial isn't going to affect anyone close to you in a bad way. This is called an 'ecology check' and we do it to make sure our action doesn't have adverse consequences for other people we are close to.

So now you know how to reframe negative experiences, let's have a go at reframing some together.

Exercise 50

Reframe the following:

→ You've just got back from work to find the cat's been run over; the trouble is that it isn't your cat. You've been looking after it for a friend. How can you reframe this?

_____

_____

_____

_____

_____

_____

→ You've lost your phone and you're expecting an important call from a new client with a big project for you. You know he can only discuss it today as he goes on holiday tomorrow. How can you reframe this?

_____

_____

_____

_____

_____

_____

➜ Your partner has told you she/he has met someone else and it's all over. You have been together for five years and were planning to start a family soon. Reframe this?

_____

_____

_____

_____

_____

➜ The holiday company you booked your cruise with has gone bust and there is no way you will get your money back. This was all your savings and the holiday of a lifetime. How can you reframe this?

_____

_____

_____

_____

_____

➜ Your boss has just told you she is very sorry but she's going to have to 'let you go' as part of departmental cuts. Reframe this?

_____

_____

_____

_____

_____

_____

How did you do? Did you manage to think up some effective reframes to turn the situations into positive ones?

· ·

Managing your state is very important in order to maintain good self-esteem. When we experience mood swings and anger outbursts, or suddenly dissolve into tears or even laugh at an inappropriate moment, our self-esteem plummets. Before we start thinking about how to control it, we need to know what your normal state is.

How are you when you are happy? Draw a picture below.

How would I be able to tell if you were happy? What would I notice about you? What would I notice about how you look, how you talk, what you say and what you do?

_____

_____

_____

_____

_____

_____

_____

Now, draw a picture of you when you are sad, angry or in a bad mood.

How would I be able to tell if you were sad or angry? What would I notice about you? What would I notice about how you look, how you talk, what you say and what you do?

_____

_____

_____

_____

_____

_____

_____

_____

This is called calibrating our state, which is basically benchmarking it, so we can easily recognize the signals for our moods and start to notice them in order to then control them.

There are several ways to control your state and you're going to learn them all so that you have a choice, because one method may appeal to you more than another or you may find one way works better for you in the situations you encounter.

Exercise 51

This is a good time to return to the subject of 'anchoring', discussed in Chapter 4. Have you heard of Pavlov's dogs? Pavlov conducted an experiment in which a bell was rung whenever the dogs were fed and after a while the dogs, on hearing the bell, expected to be fed. They started salivating and getting hungry thoughts. When only the bell was rung but no food given, their response was still the same despite the lack of food. What we want to do is find a stimulus, like the ringing bell, to create an associated response from you which will be one that you want. In this case we're going for a positive and resourceful state that enables you to feel calm and have good confidence and self-esteem.

▶ Step 1. So let's first select something to be your anchor. A bell isn't going to work is it? You can't go round with a bell in your pocket! We need a small sign or action that you can make without anyone seeing. This is what a lot of people use as their anchor.

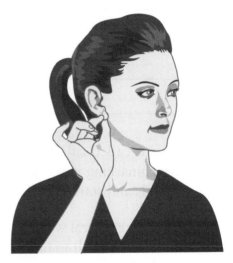

▶ Step 2. Practise it a few times so you can do it quickly and easily.

▶ Step 3. Now we need to decide what to anchor. We need a nice calm state, so close your eyes and think of a time when you felt really calm and in control. It can be a time recently or in the distant past but the sensation needs to be very powerful so pick one that really is a strong association which you can re-experience each time you use your anchor. Have you got one?

▶ Step 4. Break state for a minute. This means opening your eyes and walking around for a while so you think about something else for a minute. This takes away the intensity.

▶ Step 5. When you're ready, close your eyes again and think of that peaceful, quiet, calm time. As you imagine yourself right there, do the anchoring action you have practised. Keep the anchor while the feeling is strong but take it away as it fades.

▶ Step 6. Do this a few times and, if you like, use other memories of calm controlled times. You can change the memories but keep the anchoring action the same, and make sure it's the same type of feeling you anchor even if the actual situation is different.

Once you can access the feeling using your anchor, you can use it whenever you need to get that feeling.

Exercise 52

A variation on anchoring is the Circle of Excellence, discussed in Chapter 6, but because it is a valuable method it's worth a reminder.

→ Imagine a circle drawn on the floor, large enough to stand in. Now close your eyes and think about a time when you felt really confident. You just need to capture that feeling of being calm, confident and able to cope with anything.

→ Notice as you think about this time how your body physiology changes. Look in the mirror. Are you standing taller with your back straight and shoulders down? Some people can quickly get to their confident state just by getting themselves in the body shape that they associate with feeling confident.

→ When you are really 'into' that confident feeling, step into the circle and enjoy the feelings. This is your anchor, the step. When the feelings fade, step out and break state by giving yourself a little shake. Repeat this a few times thinking of different occasions when you felt confident.

The third method we're going to learn is the SWISH. Here's how we do this.

Exercise 53

Think about what happens just before you get into a bad mood. This is called 'the trigger'. It's like a gun; we pull the trigger in our head and 'bang' our mood changes. What we need to do is change our reaction to the trigger.

Is your trigger something you see (if you are visual), something someone says (if you are auditory) or something you feel (if you are kinaesthetic)?

Write down what happens *just before* you feel bad or angry or sad.

➡ The trigger for me is:

_____

_____

_____

_____

_____

➡ Then what happens? Write it down here.

_____

_____

_____

_____

_____

→ Make a picture in your head of what happens when you feel really bad and imagine it like a picture on the screen as if it's a movie at the cinema.

→ Now think of what you would like to happen *instead* next time that trigger goes off in your head. Write it down here.

_____

_____

_____

_____

➜ Make a picture in your head of this now and in your mind put it in the bottom left-hand corner of the screen with your bad image in the middle. Like this:

➜ Now say out loud 'SWISH'. It sometimes helps to make a movement like swatting a fly away from your face. Then make the good image in the corner switch with the bad image in the middle, like this.

You will need to practise it a few times and then you can use it every time you see, hear or feel that trigger in your head.

Now think about when you could use this technique and write your ideas below.

_____

_____

_____

_____

_____

_____

_____

Remember to use your anchor as well. You know how to anchor, so establish an anchor for feeling calm and in control and use it when you feel that you are about to get angry or sad.

→ Focus points

Take responsibility for your thinking and the behaviour that results from it by making the unconscious, conscious. You can do this by:

▶ Disassociating

▶ Anchoring a resourceful state

▶ Using clean language free of assumptions to build rapport

▶ Setting compelling outcomes for what you want to achieve

▶ Using rapport building skills

▶ Reframing, which is a great way to consciously look at a situation in a different light

▶ Swishing, which can enable you to replace unresourceful cues.

What have I learned?

→ How could I use the six-step reframe to turn around a recent negative experience?

_____

_____

_____

→ What would disassociating enable me to do?

_____

_____

_____

→ How could I tell if you liked me just by looking at you?

_____

_____

_____

→ How could I use my anchor to achieve a resourceful state for the next chapter?

_____

_____

_____

Summary

No-one can make you feel something you don't genuinely feel, and how you feel is your choice. By setting positive compelling outcomes, you can take control of how you respond. You can reframe situations or experiences to take the positive learning from them and manage your state so you can control your feelings rather than being externally referenced. Use anchoring and the SWISH for this.

Where to next?

In the next chapter you will learn all about communication: how you communicate verbally and whether you use predominantly your visual, auditory or kinaesthetic senses. Of course people can use all three, but we generally have one that overrides the others and is our default. We will naturally communicate better with those who use the same preference, but in life we also need to communicate with those who don't. By understanding all three we are best placed to switch between them to gain rapport with whoever we need to at any given time.

8 Clear communication

In this chapter you will learn:
- ▶ *How you communicate and whether you have a visual, auditory or kinaesthetic preference*
- ▶ *How to alter the way you talk in order to build rapport with someone who has a different preference*
- ▶ *The importance of smell*

In Chapter 5 we learned about VAK (visual, auditory and kinaesthetic) preferences, and we're going to explore these further in this chapter. When we are born we have access to all of our senses but, unfortunately, as we grow up we find that we can manage pretty well with just one or two and we become lazy in our use of the others. Let's recap what they are for a minute and rekindle your awareness of them.

Exercise 54

Wherever you are right now there are bound to be some **smells**. Find some and really sniff them in a few times. Make a note beside each one about what you thought of the smell and what it reminded you of, perhaps a special occasion or maybe something more everyday.

➜Coffee _____

➜Wood _____

→ Wine _____

→ Fruit _____

→ Perfume _____

→ Grass _____

→ Flowers _____

You may wonder why being aware of smell helps us communicate and how this helps with self-esteem. Yet, how often have you been put off and maybe moved away from someone smelling of cigarettes or with coffee on their breath. Are you drawn to someone who smells good? Of course you are affected by smell and you will feel more confident yourself when you know you smell nice and aren't worrying about bumping into someone just as you've left the gym all sweaty and smelly!

ANCHORING USING SMELL

Smell can be a very powerful anchor. As an unconscious anchor smells can remind us of happy times.

Case study

When I smell freshly mown grass I am immediately transported back to the field where we all played at my primary school. I can picture my friends there and remember how we threw handfuls of grass over each other laughing and chasing each other. Happy times!

My daughter loves the smell of horse manure (yes really!); it reminds her of our many cycling holidays as a family when she was young.

Smells can also remind us of sad times can't they? A particular perfume may remind us of a past love or an old friend no longer with us. Mostly though they conjure up happy memories, so how could we use them to improve our self-esteem and our communication?

How about using a favourite perfume as an anchor for confidence? When you close your eyes and remember a really good time when you were confident, resourceful and had high self-esteem, apply the perfume. If you do this a few times you will have a powerful association between the perfume and the feeling of confidence.

People generally love to be told that they smell nice. It's a good ice-breaker in a social setting to say, 'Mmm you smell good, what do you wear?', and you can say this to a man or a woman. In a social setting where you are eating, you can draw someone's attention to the smell of the food to heighten their senses and connect at a deeper level than just the surface. So instead of saying, 'Hello, what do you do?' or 'How do you know the bride and groom?' say, 'Wow! Smell that food, isn't it amazing?' and you'll have made a friend.

ANCHORING USING TASTE

Very closely associated with smell is the sense of *taste*. When you were a baby you had such a strong sense of taste that you were undoubtedly given foods which you would consider bland now. On the whole, people avoid giving babies strong or spicy foods because they fear it might be difficult to digest and an assault on their delicate taste buds. Now, however, that we are grown up, our taste buds rarely get much use. Whilst chefs who exercise their palates daily can reel out the list of ingredients in any dish just based on taste, our taste buds are quite clunky and only distinguish between very basic foods.

Case study

Last December we discussed what meat we would have on Christmas Day. I wanted goose and my brother insisted on the more traditional turkey. The meal was produced and my brother complimented us on the excellent turkey. It was goose!

Case study

I had a 70s-themed birthday party this year and served Angel Delight as the dessert. Everyone came flocking and fought over the little cups of Angel Delight with hundreds and thousands on them. They were all talking about how the taste took them back to their childhood, birthday parties and making Angel Delight at home with their mum.

Taste too can conjure up memories, both happy and sad.

Exercise 55

Choose a few of your favourite foods, then close your eyes and taste them. We eat with our eyes and our sense of smell so what do our favourite foods taste like when we don't see them first?

→ Any surprises? Make a note here:

_____

_____

_____

_____

_____

···

Becoming more aware of your taste and smell senses will make you more aware of other senses too and we'll talk about them now.

ANCHORING USING VISION

Let's start with our **visual** sense. You're using this now to read this book and you're noticing the words, the layout and the pictures. If this is your preferred way of processing then you are generally very aware of what you see around you and how you look. You notice how things look, the design element and the shape, colours and texture. When you communicate you use words that have a visual context such as 'view', 'see', 'look', 'watch'. You will be aware of how you look and this will affect your mood or state. You'll also really notice what other people around you are wearing. You'll be more aware than most of their facial expressions and their body language because you're observant. So how does this affect how you communicate?

You speak fast as you gather the images in your head and try to put them into words, and your pitch is quite excited and high. This means that a non-visual listener might struggle to follow what you're saying. So SLOW DOWN! Reduce your speed so people can follow you, and take your pitch down so it sounds calmer and less frenetic. People will relate better to you if they can understand what you're saying and have the opportunity to contribute, so pause and let them speak. Ask what they think and be curious about their point of view.

Exercise 56

Imagine you are not a visual person. How would you change how you communicate in order to connect with someone visual?

_____

_____

_____

_____

_____

If you are in a meeting with visual people, say people from a design agency, graphics, advertising or other arty function, you would apply these rules to them too of course. They will particularly appreciate presentations that are more visual than auditory and have plenty of visual material, collages, film, photos, images and diagrams. Express visually what you want to say and you will be on their wavelength.

Check this out by asking, 'Can you see what I'm saying?', 'Can you see where I'm coming from?' or 'Can you see it from the consumer's point of view?' because these are all visual questions.

ANCHORING USING SOUND

Now let's move on to the **auditory** preference.

You are more auditory if you tend to speak quite slowly and carefully, paying attention to the words you use and what people say. This means that you will enjoy talking to people, and you're a good listener too which is a great start when it comes to clear communication.

When you are talking to another auditory person others may not get a look in! When you're talking with non-auditory people you need to cut your sentences down a bit because they may not be prepared to hear you out and will jump in with their own thoughts and ideas. They're not being rude, they just don't value conversation as much as you do and want to speed up the process. Tune in to your visual skills and watch for when they want to say something and notice their body language.

Your voice is lower in pitch than a visual person's, and slightly more monotone than a kinaesthetic person's, so to hold someone's attention you may need to vary the tone and make your pitch slightly higher. Use changes of pace to maintain interest in the subject and where appropriate use hand gestures. If you are giving a talk or a presentation remember to use visual aids to hold the interest of your audience.

You may be musical and enjoy listening to music, perhaps playing a musical instrument. Harmonious sounds will be pleasurable, but you will be more offended than most by music and sounds you don't want around you such as traffic noise, machine noise or discordant music. You can control your auditory environment by using an mp3 player to listen to your own choice of music in some situations but not all. When it gets too much, use an anchor to stay calm and relaxed. Music may well be a good anchor, so put music on your player that you find calming or, if you need to be motivated or uplifted, choose music that lifts your mood.

My Dad is auditory and talks a lot! He enjoys conversation
but finds silence unsettling so he fills it, which means that
there is often no thinking time for other people to make
a considered response. Although he listens fairly well, he
is almost immediately forming his next sentence as one
tries to respond to the last one! This leads to a monologue
situation unless one is very careful, so a tried and tested
method of interjecting is to say, 'Dad can I say something?'
and this usually stops him in his tracks.

Auditory people use words like 'sound', 'hear' 'listen' 'noise'
and say things like, 'That's music to my ears' or 'I like the
sound of that' or 'I don't like what I'm hearing'. When you
want to get the attention of an auditory person you need to
say something like, 'Listen to this I...' or 'What I want to say
is...' or 'I want to tell you about...'.

Exercise 57

Imagine you are communicating with an auditory
person. How will you adjust your own way of speaking
so you have their attention?

_____

_____

_____

_____

_____

ANCHORING USING ACTION

The **kinaesthetic** preference is possibly the easiest to spot quickly because kinaesthetic people tend to move quite a bit. They fidget a lot and don't sit or stand still. They are often active sporty people who enjoy being energetic, but because they like doing things and being practical they could be in a practical job, making things or working with materials.

They talk with their whole body using hand and whole-body gestures and could well be doing something while they are talking and appearing not to give you full attention. There is usually a lot of energy in their voice, but they don't talk as much as an auditory or visual person as they tend to think that actions speak louder than words. They may well touch you on the arm or shoulder when they speak to you to emphasize their connection to you and they will stand close to you, possibly touching. If you want to connect with a kinaesthetic don't move away too obviously if you're uncomfortable with this.

Case study

My husband is kinaesthetic. He takes every opportunity to exercise, cycling to the station and back every day and takes a walk at lunchtime. He can't sit still for very long and fidgets non-stop! He'll never whisper sweet nothings in my ear, enjoy a good natter over a glass of wine or notice if I look nice but he's always doing things for me and for the family as his way of showing his love.

Kinaesthetic people talk about 'getting to grips' with something, and 'getting a handle' on it; they will use words like 'make' and 'do', which are action and feeling words. They prefer to meet up with people face to face rather than connect by email and text, and they like to be doing something rather than just talking so kinaesthetics are likely to combine business with golf or sport. They like workshops and team-building days and opportunities to get involved in what they are doing.

Exercise 58

Let's assume you've just been introduced to a potential new client. You suspect she is kinaesthetic as you've spotted her gym bag near her desk and she's touching her colleague's shoulder as she speaks with him. She's turning to greet you. How do you connect? What are you going to say and how will you impress on her that you are on her wavelength?

_____

_____

_____

_____

→ Focus points

▶ If you tend to prefer visual communication you will probably talk fast, madly trying to capture those visual images in your brain and communicate them in speech.

▶ If you are auditory, your speech will be slower and more thoughtful as you select just the right words to express your thoughts.

▶ If you are kinaesthetic you will speak in quite a lively way with a lot of hand and body gestures.

▶ Get to become an expert at quickly assessing the preference of the person you are talking to so you can talk their language and get into rapport. You will gain confidence and self-esteem from the rapport-rich connections you make.

What have I learned?

→ What preference is my partner? How can I use this knowledge to ask him/her to do something they don't really want to do?

_____

_____

_____

→ How would I engage with a kinaesthetic person?

_____

_____

_____

→ If I was presenting material to a group of musicians how would I ensure their engagement?

_____

_____

_____

Summary

This chapter has given you the opportunity to consider how to adapt your communication depending on who you are talking to and bearing in mind their VAK and your own.

The watchword is flexibility. We tend to use the same communication style with everyone, only being flexible perhaps in the area of formality as we change our language pattern and body language depending on whether we are talking to someone we know well, someone senior to us at work or someone who reports to us.

In this chapter you have been invited to consider making more changes based on VAK. This will take some practising and as you practise and connect more in rapport with the people around you this will increase your self-esteem as you realize how adaptable you can be and how, by using your new skills, you can achieve rapport with anyone you choose.

Where to next?

Frequently throughout this workbook the importance of taking responsibility for your own thinking and becoming aware of how that thinking is affecting your behaviour has been emphasized. Intrinsic to this is the aspect of becoming internally referenced. In the next chapter we'll explore how, instead of constantly bouncing back from other people's perceptions of you, you can instead be your own judge of what is right and wrong according to your own set of values and beliefs.

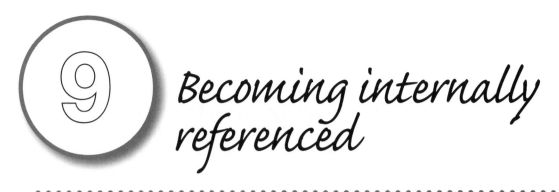

Becoming internally referenced

In this chapter you will learn:
▶ *To what extent you rely on others to give you confidence*
▶ *How constantly comparing yourself to others can affect your self-esteem*
▶ *How to become 'internally referenced'*

We have already learned the difference between internal and external referencing, and in this chapter we will explore it in more detail. To refresh your memory: when we compare and contrast ourselves with 'other people', then we are externally referenced, and when we don't and rely on our own internal judgement based on our values and beliefs, then we are internally referenced.

We also learned about matching and mismatching; we match when we compare what we have in common with other people and mismatch when we notice what is different. When we combine these two meta-programmes we can see how they might affect our self-esteem.

▶ **Matching/external** – when we look at what we have in common with others this is a healthy way to be respectful and look for opportunities to achieve a rapport. We are comparing ourselves with others by looking for things we have in common and this will lead to very agreeable communications with each person agreeing with the other – 'whatever you say'. Of course, this may not be entirely genuine common ground because the emphasis is on being agreeable rather than expressing what you genuinely feel so, whilst you may get a temporary sense of high self-esteem due to the good feeling generated by the interaction, you may afterwards wonder whether you actually presented yourself and your views or just reflected back theirs.

▶ **Mismatching/external** – here we are looking at how we are different from others either positively or negatively and the resulting communications will not be in rapport because there will be constant differences of opinion. In this situation you are very aware of the other person's views and want to counter them with different ones of your own. This can lead to a lively debate and may be a challenging situation. You may feel you have high self-esteem because you are expressing your opinions and you are, in some ways, in rapport because you are listening and taking on board what the other person is saying. It can be very wearing though and not everyone likes these 'let's agree to disagree' types of discussion.

▶ **Matching/internal** – we aren't looking to match because we are less aware of the other person, so the interactions will be more authentic as there is genuinely common ground. Views are more likely to be based on deeply held beliefs and values and because you both hold them, the matching will make the interaction intense. You will feel high self-esteem because you will feel you are being genuine, that your views are being heard and agreed with and that the other person likes you – 'that's just how I feel too'.

▶ **Mismatching/internal** – we don't really care about the other person's needs and just want to be disagreeable and find points of difference. This is not likely to be a successful interaction and is the behaviour of a bully. In the unlikely event that you ever behave like this, it may give you a temporary sense of high self-esteem, but is not going to be sustainable long term and won't give you a good sense of self-worth – 'I don't care what you think and anyway you're wrong'.

We can match or mismatch visually by how we dress and how we place ourselves (see Chapter 6 on body language, for a reminder); in an auditory style (see the previous examples) or kinaesthetically by what we actually do.

Exercise 59

How internally or externally referenced are you when it comes to what you wear? Answer these questions honestly!

1 Do you usually check with your friends what they are wearing before you go out?

a Usually

b Sometimes if it's an important 'do'

c Never

2 Do you go shopping with a friend/partner so they can give their opinion before you buy something?

a Yes usually

b Only for special occasion clothes

c No I shop alone

3 If someone doesn't compliment you on your new outfit what do you do?

a Never wear it again

b Decide they are rude

c Doesn't bother me at all

4 **Do you ask other people where they buy their clothes?**

   a Yes because I want to shop there too

   b No because I shop where I want

   c Sometimes if I like what they are wearing

5 **How long do you spend deciding what to wear on an a working day?**

   a Less than ten minutes

   b Around half an hour

   c It varies

6 **Do you wear similar clothes to your work colleagues?**

   a Yes I usually do

   b No I like to stand out and look different

   c I hadn't noticed

7 **Who do you dress for?**

   a Others

   b Myself

   c No-one

8 **Do your clothes reflect your mood or personality?**

   a Never thought about it

   b Usually

   c No

9 Do you compliment others on their clothes?

   a Yes because I want them to notice mine

   b No because I don't care what they're wearing

   c Yes because it's polite

10 Do you ask your friends what they think of what you're wearing?

   a Yes if they haven't commented already

   b Yes because I want to know what they think

   c No, it doesn't matter what they think

You can easily work out whether you are internally or externally referenced from your answers I think! The 'a' answers suggest external referencing and 'b' is internal. If you've answered 'c' then go back and think again! Remember it is a sliding scale so your answers may well vary according to the type of occasion and who matters to you. The thing to bear in mind is that you become aware of who you are seeking approval from and make sure you check in with yourself during this process rather than relying totally on other people's opinions.

Case study

My daughter was attending the wedding of her boyfriend's sister. It involved a church marriage ceremony first, then a reception, so she wanted to choose a dress that would be appropriate in both environments. She also wanted to please her boyfriend and his family so it could not be too outrageous. She is externally referenced and sent links to a number of possible outfits to her boyfriend to get his opinion and then took him shopping to get the dress and accessories.

One of the reasons why being internally referenced will increase your self-esteem is that it guards against the idiosyncrasies of other people's judgements. Imagine if you spent your time and energy on trying to get everyone's approval for what you say and do (and wear)? People have different opinions so would you have to change yours to match theirs to gain their approval? Wouldn't this mean that you'd be expressing contradictory opinions all the time, such that you'd end up losing track of what your own opinion was?

Instead, decide what you think based on your own values and beliefs and express it, being conscious that other people have different opinions. So instead of taking any disagreement as a personal attack, be curious about how other people think about the issue and you may even change your opinion.

Being internally referenced is about holding on to what you believe to be true rather than taking on other people's views, and standing up for what you believe in and value while recognizing that this may be different from someone else's. This does not mean you are wrong or that they are, just that you are both different.

When we are internally referenced, we constantly check in with ourselves, asking ourselves, 'What do I think about this?' rather than simply echoing the views of others. In a group of friends with whom you are usually in agreement, you may suddenly find that you feel uncomfortable about a decision that has been made or an opinion that has been expressed. In that situation you need to stop and say to yourself, 'Hang on, I just want to have a think about that'.

Case study

I was once working for a market research agency where one part of the business was very profitable (the one I worked in) but the other was not. The head of the profitable team decided to break away and set up a separate company. I felt uncomfortable about this because it had been the MD who was also head of the unprofitable business who had trained me and I felt it was disloyal to leave. It was an unpopular decision and I was the only one who decided not to leave. The profitable team went on to become hugely successful. Nevertheless I still believe I made the decision that sat easiest on my shoulders, even though the natural choice would have been to go with my colleagues.

When you are working with externally referenced colleagues and sense that they have not internalized an issue, ask them, 'What do you think?' or 'What is your view on this?' If you are working with internally referenced colleagues and believe they have not considered other people's views then ask, 'What does the rest of your team think about this?' or 'Is that a majority view?' or 'Are you speaking for the team on this one?'

Teenagers and young people can be externally referenced in their desire to gain the approval of their peers. Use the same questioning to encourage them to internalize.

Sustainable self-esteem derives from being internally referenced to the extent that you know your own skills and strengths and love the person you are, but not without regard to what other people think. You are aware of other people, interested in their views and influenced by them but not overruled by them. You may allow yourself to be persuaded to do something they want to do more than you do but not if it means going against your principles.

→ Focus points

▶ Look for what you have in common with others and opportunities to be in rapport.

▶ Find areas of agreement and, rather than seek to change their opinion, be curious about it and wonder where the common ground might be.

▶ Once you've found it, you will soon find other similarities and stay in rapport without losing touch with your own values and beliefs.

▶ You never know; maybe you'll amend a belief you've had for a while based on new information or other people's experiences.

What have I learned?

➔ What percentage of the time do I think I am externally referenced compared to internally referenced?

_____

_____

_____

➔ What difference would it make to my life if I increased the amount of time I was internally referenced?

_____

_____

_____

➔ Of my colleagues or friends, think of one person who seems very externally referenced and another who is very internally referenced.

_____

_____

_____

Summary

If you are externally referenced then you rely on others rather than making decisions based on your own values and beliefs; this can be dangerous because you can be drawn in directions not of your choosing, unsure what is the right thing to do. Being internally referenced means that you check in with your own values and beliefs and convey them. Flexibility is key though. It is important to be able to both internally and externally reference to build rapport and self-esteem.

Where to next?

The drama triangle is a situation where roles are adopted: victim, persecutor and rescuer. According to Eric Berne (founder of Transactional Analysis) this game starts in childhood where children play the role of victim to the parents' rescuer. The rescuer after a while turns persecutor as they become increasingly frustrated with rescuing. The problem with the game is that these roles are often taken into adult life and the victim never takes responsibility for their actions thereby perpetuating the game. Learn how you can step away from the drama triangle in the next chapter.

10 *The drama triangle*

• •

In this chapter you will learn:
▶ *About the roles of the victim, rescuer and persecutor, so that you can identify times in your life when you adopt them*
▶ *How to recognize the ever changing triangle as people switch roles*
▶ *How to exit the triangle*

• •

Do you sometimes think 'poor me' and feel that the whole world is against you? Maybe you think you're unlucky and nothing ever works out right for you? Do you often feel guilty even though you know it wasn't your fault? This is the 'victim' orientation in Stephen Karpman's drama triangle and this orientation is the polar opposite of high self-esteem, which is why we're going to learn about it in this chapter. Find out how you can change this pattern.

As you near the end of the book and have completed many exercises on self-esteem, you will by now have discovered a great deal more about yourself than you previously knew. You will also have increased your self-esteem and be able to feel confident and assertive in most, if not all, situations. However, even the most confident person can have an Achilles' heel. Even very powerful people can be reduced to a mumbling wreck in the presence of their mother or an older sibling, their spouse or partner.

Perhaps it's your boss you fear or the managing director? In some situations even people with high self-esteem can find themselves at a disadvantage because they put themselves, unwittingly perhaps, in the role of victim in a 'drama triangle'.

Perhaps you are the person always ready and willing to help out, the one there with the box of tissues and the cup of tea? Or are you sometimes the persecutor, blaming others, hiding your feelings and manipulating people around you? None of us take these roles constantly but move around the triangle taking different roles as the drama unfolds. Here's how it works.

A drama triangle occurs when there are three people taking the roles of victim, persecutor and rescuer. As the drama unfolds, the roles change as they move round the triangle.

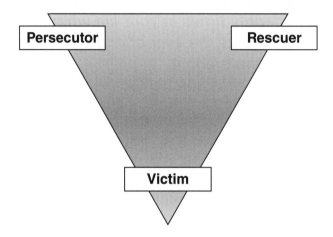

Let's start with the central role, the victim, sometimes called 'poor me'. The victim comes about as a result of other people (in the persecutor role) or situations acting upon them, which they feel unable to do anything about. This could be a natural disaster such as a volcanic eruption, earthquake, train crash, etc. It could be an illness, disability, being old or it could just be the traffic, train delays or the weather. It can be other people: your boss, partner, the kids, a work colleague, the teacher, etc. We all experience the same situations in life but how we respond is what makes the difference. You are only a 'victim' if you choose to be.

When you look for someone to blame, feel needy and vulnerable and believe you can't do anything yourself then you have taken the victim role. You look for someone to help you, show you what to do and listen to your troubles.

At first you are grateful for the rescuer's help but after a while you end up feeling resentful and undermined. You then have three options:

▶ FIGHT – you become the persecutor

▶ FLIGHT – you head off in search of another rescuer

▶ FREEZE – you numb the pain through work, food or drink.

Here are some typical traits of the victim: defensive, overly sensitive, manipulative, submissive. Do you ever say anything like this?

Exercise 60

Which of the above have you said recently? Think back to the occasion and write down what happened, what you said and how you felt...

→ Just before _____

→ During _____

→ Afterwards _____

All victims feel they have been thwarted in some way; they have been prevented from achieving their dream. Of course, it was not their fault. Do you feel like this sometimes? Think about when you last felt like this and answer these questions about the occasion.

➡Who were you blaming?

_____

_____

_____

_____

➡Why them?

_____

_____

_____

_____

➡What other choices did you have?

_____

_____

_____

_____

➡What other choices do you have now?

_____

_____

_____

_____

➡Are you ready to make these choices?

_____

_____

_____

_____

So what about the victim? The victim is the person who decides that they are the victim, they are needy and vulnerable and they believe they can't do anything themselves so they have to look for someone to help them. They usually feel inadequate and look for someone to rescue them, help them out, show them what to do and listen to their troubles. At first they are grateful for the rescuer's help but after a while they feel resentful and undermined and they become the persecutor, although inside they still feel like the victim because they feel inadequate and have low self-esteem.

In families one often sees a triangle where the child takes it upon themselves to be the victim. Mum rescues. Dad then decides he can't have this and turns into the persecutor to get the child to 'man up' and take some responsibility. The more he persecutes, the more Mum will rescue and the more helpless the child will feel, especially as Dad may persecute Mum for rescuing, so Mum becomes the victim. Now the child tries to rescue Mum for which he'll probably be persecuted by Dad. These childhood patterns can unfortunately be continued into adulthood, as victim children become victim teenagers seeking out a persecutor in the form of an abusive relationship.

So the pattern continues as the victim goes from being the scapegoat in the family scenario to being bullied at school and being picked on at work. But why? Well this behaviour gets attention which many victims confuse with love. The pattern is almost subconscious because victims don't deliberately set out to evoke sympathy in return for attention or to seek relationships that reinforce the pattern.

What do you do if you identify with this pattern? You have already made the first step if you recognize it in yourself. The next step is to use the exercises in this workbook to raise your self-esteem and start to take responsibility for your own confidence rather than looking to others to 'make you' feel good about yourself. You need to internally reference and learn to appreciate your skills and qualities. In this way you won't need to be rescued, which puts the potential rescuer out of a job! You can then exit the triangle.

Exercise 61

Whether you identify with the victim role or know someone who behaves in this way, do this exercise to explore ways to exit the triangle.

Think of a situation where you have (perhaps without being aware of it at the time) put yourself in the victim role. Write about it here.

_____

_____

_____

_____

_____

_____

→ Who took the role of rescuer?

_____

_____

_____

_____

_____

→ What did they do?

_____

_____

_____

_____

_____

→ What did they say?

_____

_____

_____

_____

_____

→ Who took the role of persecutor?

_____

_____

_____

_____

_____

→ What did they do?

_____

_____

_____

_____

_____

→ What did they say?

_____

_____

_____

_____

→ Did you move into the persecutor role?

_____

_____

_____

_____

→ In what way? How did you do that?

Now think about what you could do differently when that situation happens again. How could you take responsibility and exit the triangle?

_____

_____

_____

_____

Something to be aware of in the victim role is that co-dependency tends to lead to addictive behaviour and unhealthy relationships. When you are in the victim role you feel out of control and the more out of control you feel, the more you are likely to drink, smoke or eat. You are also more likely to be ill because of this behaviour, and because you aren't taking control of your health. Many workaholics are victims addicted to work.

Let's move on to the rescuer orientation because this is not all it would appear. The rescuer, sometimes called 'Poor you', steps in between the victim and the persecutor, ostensibly to 'help'; and what is wrong with that, you might ask? But, the rescuer prevents the victim from solving the problem themselves, thus increasing their self-esteem, by snatching it away from them because 'they can't do it for themselves'.

The rescuer could be a person but it can also be alcohol, work, food, drugs, etc. The rescuer actually boosts their self-esteem from attempting to fix the problem and having people dependent on them. Their positive intention is to improve their self-esteem by being important and helping rather than having a genuine desire to help. They seek out people weaker than themselves, needier, more dependent and they keep the victim in this dependent state by taking care of them. They consciously seek to find someone to rescue in order to feel important; they believe they have all the answers. They volunteer for everything but then feel resentful and 'put upon' and frequently switch to persecutor role.

Rescuers are often first or only children who have perhaps looked after younger siblings at an early age. They could be from a dysfunctional family where they have had to take responsibility for a disabled child or abused/addict mother.

Many mothers put themselves into rescuer orientation because they believe their child to be a potential victim, unable to manage things for themselves. But all is not as it seems because some parents rely on this role to feed their own self-esteem.

Case study

Karen does everything for her children; she is overprotective and the children can do nothing for themselves even though they are old enough to do so. She is busy from morning to night and even after they've gone to bed she makes their packed lunches, gets their clothes ready for the morning, packs their school bags and tidies the lounge of their mess. They are 10 and 12! She resents what she does and frequently shouts at them when she gets tired. Any attempt they make to take responsibility themselves is met with criticism and she redoes whatever they've attempted the 'right way' because they have done it 'wrong'. Karen spends her life moving round the triangle from rescuer to 'poor me' victim to persecutor, then back again to rescuer and so on. When she learns to allow her children to take responsibility and learn from their mistakes she will exit the triangle.

The rescuer enjoys manipulating people into feeling guilty and dependent on them. They will say whatever needs to be said to keep everyone happy and avoid any negative attention on them. Do you ever say or think like this?

Exercise 62

Which of the above have you said recently?

➜ Ask yourself, what did I get out of this? What was my positive intention, honestly!?

_____

_____

_____

_____

_____

➜ What could you have done or said differently that would still have given you a positive outcome?

_____

_____

_____

_____

_____

➜ What would have to be true for you to be able to hand over responsibility to someone else?

_____

_____

_____

_____

_____

Have you heard the expression, 'Give a man a fish and he will eat for a day; teach him to fish and he can feed himself for the rest of his life.' This is what rescuers need to be aware of and act upon, because otherwise they can suffer stress through suppressed anger at constantly taking on responsibility for the problems of others. This can lead to illness and addictive behaviour in order to numb the anger.

Let's conclude with the persecutor role , 'win at any cost'. So how do we recognize the persecutor? Persecutors often start out as victims, feeling out of control and lacking self-esteem. No-one is listening to them because they are not expressing their needs clearly and assertively. They don't believe that what they have to say is important and give responsibility to those around them rather than taking it on for themselves. They take out their frustration on others, blaming and criticizing.

These are people who separate themselves, even temporarily, from their emotions and distance themselves. They blame everyone else for the situation they are in and when you ask them what's the matter they say 'nothing'. In the persecutor role they are angry, either overtly or passively aggressive. They fear loss of control where the rescuer fears a loss of purpose.

Do you say any of these things?

Persecutors want to control and do this by nagging, putting others down and humiliating people. We've probably all done this at one time or another. Have you?

Exercise 63

Think of a time when you have been a persecutor. Remember it is the flip side of being a victim, so you may have experienced this switch just before you took on the persecutor role. Write down how it happened.

_____

_____

_____

_____

_____

_____

_____

Now think about how you could have handled the situation differently and exited the triangle without moving into the persecutor role. What could you have said or done? Write it here.

_____

_____

_____

_____

_____

_____

_____

_____

_____

_____

· ·

A typical persecutor/victim that we see daily as parents is
two children squabbling. One blames the other for taking
their toy and the younger child cries and runs to Mummy,
the rescuer. But the persecutor feels they are the victim;
it was their toy that was taken so they become the victim
and Mum becomes the persecutor telling them off, and the
younger child now becomes rescuer comforting the older
child. Here are some other examples.

Case study

As a busy working mum I do loads for my kids, far more
than I need to, in fact. I ask them to help but then before
they do anything, I do the job myself and get cross at them
for not helping. I make all the arrangements for our social
life, never asking my husband to do anything and then
get annoyed that I have no surprises and have booked all
our holidays and so on. Whilst on the surface I am the
rescuer helping everyone and doing everything, I feel like
the victim ('poor me') and behave as a persecutor, blaming
everyone for not helping.

Does this sound familiar?! Here's a work based example.

Case study

Jenny gets in early every day so that she keeps on top of her workload. She will help anyone who needs help with the new software the company has just installed and she remembers everyone's birthday. She listens to her colleagues moaning about their boss or their partner and rarely shares her own problems. She is in rescuer mode and everyone loves her; this is how she likes it. But she feels like a victim because she is not appreciated; people have become accustomed to her being there to help and now she feels taken advantage of. She has started to snap at her boss when she asks her for help and has become the persecutor in that relationship.

You've probably experienced similar situations yourself at home or at work or maybe in your social life. In the following exercise you will have a go at working out the roles played by each person at each stage.

Exercise 64

Think of a time when you felt like a victim, persecutor or rescuer and work around the triangle sorting out who played what roles and what you observed that tells you that their behaviour was typical of that role.

→Stage 1

_____

_____

_____

_____

_____

➜Stage 2

_____

_____

_____

_____

_____

➜Stage 3

_____

_____

_____

_____

_____

➜Stage 4

_____

_____

_____

_____

_____

➜ Stage 5

_____

_____

_____

_____

_____

_____

➜ Stage 6

_____

_____

_____

_____

_____

_____

There don't have to be six stages: there might be
more, but six gives you the chance to go round the
triangle twice and experience how the roles keep
changing.

· ·

You don't need other people in the triangle in order to
experience this for yourself. In fact when you have low self-
esteem this is often how it works.

You feel inadequate; perhaps you've made a silly mistake at work. It's not the first time and you think about other things you've done wrong. You feel like a victim and feel sorry for yourself. Then you decide that this is ridiculous and tell yourself to 'pull yourself together and just get on with it'; in other words, you rescue yourself. Then you get annoyed with yourself for being so pathetic, so you persecute yourself. You then return to being a victim, and so on round the triangle you go.

Have you experienced this type of situation?

Exercise 65

Think of a time when you felt like a victim, rescuer and persecutor in a recent situation. What happened and what were the different roles?

→Stage 1

_____

_____

_____

_____

_____

→Stage 2

_____

_____

_____

→ Stage 3

_____

_____

_____

_____

_____

→ Stage 4

_____

_____

_____

_____

_____

→ Stage 5

_____

_____

_____

_____

_____

_____

_____

_____

_____

_____

· ·

Many fairy stories are based on this triangle. For example, in *Cinderella* the Fairy Godmother is the rescuer, Cinderella is the victim and the stepmother and step sisters are persecutors. Who are you?! There is usually a knight in shining armour on a white charger who comes to rescue the victim from the wicked witch or stepmother, and many women search in vain for their knight when, by stepping out of the triangle, they would find that they don't need to be rescued at all.

→ Stepping out of the triangle

Here are the steps to breaking out of this triangle:

1 Be aware that you are in it by recognizing the patterns. What are the triggers? What happens before? Is the trigger visual, auditory or kinaesthetic? How do you set up the trigger? Do you consciously or unconsciously manipulate the situation?

2 STOP IT! Decide now to break free of this drama triangle; step outside it.

3 Imagine you could float above the triangle and observe what's happening, who is saying and doing what. This is disassociating and allows you to emotionally distance yourself from what is going on.

4 From this place outside the triangle recognize your key role in it.

5 What is your positive intention? What do you really want? What is the compelling outcome you have set for yourself?

6 Internally reference by asking yourself, 'What are my values?', 'What are my qualities?', 'What makes me a worthwhile human being?'

7 Accept that you can change and take responsibility for yourself.

8 Live in the moment and express yourself and your needs openly and honestly.

9 Be curious about how you can live differently and be open to change, observing how others respond to you when you are outside of the triangle.

10 Be prepared to make a few mistakes along the way – there is no failure, only feedback.

→ Focus points

▶ This chapter has brought to your awareness situations where you may put yourself into the role of the victim ('poor me'), persecutor ('it's your fault') or rescuer ('let me help you').

▶ Ask yourself if you follow a pattern and if, by stepping out of the triangle, you will enable someone else to become responsible and find their own solution.

▶ When you are free of the triangle, you are also free to become aligned to your own values and achieve your own compelling outcome rather than becoming embroiled in someone else's.

What have I learned?

→ When I have been in the role of victim, how could I have exited the triangle by taking responsibility?

_____

_____

_____

→ When in the rescuer role, how could I have left the victim to take responsibility for themselves?

_____

_____

_____

→ When in the persecutor role, do I recognize that by exiting the triangle I would have encouraged others to take responsibility for their actions?

_____

_____

_____

Summary

The drama triangle has three roles or positions: rescuer, victim and persecutor. In any situation one can switch roles, but essentially the triangle remains. The ideal is to be able to recognize when you are in a drama triangle, recognize who is taking which roles and when they switch, then take action to exit the triangle by understanding the positive intention of each role and allowing others to take responsibility for their own actions.

Exercise 66

Phew! Well done for completing all the exercises! The book has been a very thorough exploration of self-esteem and by now I hope you have mastered how to improve your self-esteem and are able to share this new knowledge and your discoveries with your friends and colleagues. No doubt they have noticed a difference in you. Let's put it to the test and compare your answers with those in Exercise 1, now that you've read the book.

→ How well do you take criticism? ☐

→ Do you feel valued by your colleagues or those you interact with daily? ☐

→ How often do you say what you really think or do you just agree with the majority view? ☐

→ Do you get what you want from your relationships? ☐

→ Do you take it personally if someone doesn't agree with you? ☐

→ Are you envious of what others have and think they're doing better than you? ☐

→ Do you sometimes feel unloved? ☐

→ Do you feel embarrassed about your appearance? ☐

→ Do you sometimes feel like a victim? ☐

→ Do you feel you're not good enough? ☐

Look back to see how much these scores have changed. A lot, I'm sure.

Use the space below to take a moment to disassociate and view yourself as others might see you. How much have you changed and how would others recognize this? Perhaps people have already commented. Are you looking and asking for feedback? Feedback is on-going and is your way of checking how you're doing against the benchmark of your compelling outcomes and your values.

_____

_____

_____

_____

_____

_____

_____

_____

_____

_____

11 Applying what you've learned

► *How to apply self-esteem skills to achieve the results you want in different areas of your life.*

So now you have the self-esteem skills, how can you apply them in your everyday life? We've talked quite a bit about applying them at work, but life isn't all work and no play is it? We have other roles as parents, partners, sportspeople and so on, and we'll now look at applying your new skills in these roles.

PARENTS

As a parent you will be applying self-esteem in two ways: to manage your role as a parent of your children and also to act as a role model of self-esteem for your child. How can they learn to have high self-esteem if they don't see it demonstrated?

Having read the book, how do you think you are now demonstrating high self-esteem? What are you doing or saying differently?

_____

_____

_____

_____

_____

_____

_____

_____

_____

_____

_____

_____

_____

How is this affecting how you feel as a parent? Are you happier, more in control, calmer?

As a parent you need your children to do what you've asked and to follow guidelines that you have set, whatever age they are. We have spoken about VAK and the meta-programmes and you can use this knowledge to work out which preference your child has so you can choose language that resonates with them.

Let's assume you want to get your visual child to eat their vegetables: you would focus on making them look attractive, using combinations of colour such as carrots and peas and arranging them in a way that looks appealing on the plate. Very young children would enjoy a picture. A kinaesthetic child might enjoy eating them with chopsticks and an auditory child might enjoy crunchy vegetables.

Instruct them using their preference so, for a visual child you might say, 'Look at how well you're eating your vegetables' or 'Let's see how many peas you can eat'. An auditory child would respond to, 'I'd like to hear that you've finished all your vegetables' or counting them as they eat them. A kinaesthetic child will respond to, 'You're doing really well'. Focus on what they are eating rather than what's not being eaten.

Choice of words is really important, so avoid using 'if' when they have no choice, e.g. instead of saying, 'If you eat your vegetables you can have a...' say 'When you've eaten your vegetables...' which assumes they will eat them. Only use 'if' when they do have a genuine choice. The word 'but' emphasizes everything after it, so when you praise them do not add a 'but' because it will cancel out the praise, e.g. 'I'm really pleased you've brushed your teeth, but could you please hurry up and get to bed', does not work as effectively as 'Will you please hurry up and get to bed, but I'm really pleased you've brushed your teeth'.

'Don't' is another word that doesn't work with children as it simply suggests what they could do or will do. When we say 'Don't drop that!' they probably will, so say instead, 'Hold it carefully'. As parents we often ask our child to 'try' to do something, but don't you actually just want them to 'do it'? Be clear and just tell them. 'Yes tags' are really useful with children, so assume they want to do what you've asked and then add a 'yes tag', e.g. 'I'm sure you'd like to get your homework done before tea wouldn't you?'

Which strategy will you try?

_____

_____

_____

_____

_____

We talked in Chapter 10 about the drama triangle, and we mentioned how parents can easily switch from victim or rescuer into the persecutor role. To avoid this, step away from the triangle altogether by encouraging children to take responsibility for themselves, even if you have to show extreme patience!

Use anchoring to get that calm state when you sense you're getting frazzled and stay resourceful. Anchor a time when you feel or felt completely in control and use that anchor whenever you need it.

The knowledge about giving and receiving feedback will be extremely useful as parenting is continual feedback, isn't it? Never allow yourself to feel a failure; every situation has a learning opportunity so look for the positive intention in what your child has done and learn from it. Show them how to get the positive intention without the negative behaviour. For example, your child is throwing a tantrum in the middle of the supermarket. He is probably bored and tired and just wants a hug. He doesn't realize that, so instead of getting angry you need to do the opposite. Give him a hug and the attention he needs. There is no point trying to reason with a child who is having a tantrum. Use feedback sandwiches so they get the learning in between the praise and affirmation.

You can use your reframe skills to show them how to turn something that initially seemed really bad into something that has a positive spin, e.g. 'I know your best friend has moved, but you'll have more time to play with your other friends now, won't you?' Note the 'yes tag' and the use of 'but' to emphasize the positive spin. Children love to SWISH and you can show them how to use this to change negative situations into positive ones.

Show children how to be internally referenced when they are being led astray by other children at school. Ask them 'And what do *you* think?' Disassociation is a great gift in parenting as it helps you to separate yourself from the emotion of a situation. Imagine you are an impartial observer watching the situation or argument: what would they suggest you do or say?

The most important use of your self-esteem though is to act as a role model for your child. Do as you want them to do and show that you can keep calm, be confident and use your physiology to make the point. No-one has ever influenced a child from another room holding the belief that it will work, because it won't. Use eye contact and a confident physiology.

If you haven't got it, then disappear for a moment – use your anchor and come back with the right physiology. Remember YOU are the message before you've even said a word. Think about how you model the behaviour you want from your child. When you experience behaviour you don't like, ask yourself 'How do I do this?' They have learned the behaviour so, whilst they may apply it in a different way in different situations, you modelled it in the first place. This is, of course, also true of positive behaviour!

Ask yourself now, how could you deliberately model what you want to see in your child?

_____

_____

_____

_____

_____

Lots of parents who bring their children to me with low self-esteem also have low self-esteem themselves; this is how they recognize it and yet they don't realize where it came from. Now that you have worked through this book I hope you are now modelling high self-esteem for your child to learn. What differences are you noticing in them?

_____

_____

_____

_____

_____

You have the opportunity to apply what you have learned to give your child the gift of good self-esteem; a gift that will ensure that they make the very best of every opportunity available to them.

MARRIAGE/PARTNERSHIPS

Good self-esteem in your relationship is essential so that you can express your needs and your feelings. If you previously found yourself saying 'yes' when you meant 'no', or constantly apologizing and not getting what you needed from your relationship, then what you have learned in this book will be invaluable. Have you already started to notice changes in the dynamics of your relationship? Note them here:

_____

_____

_____

_____

Have you worked out your partner's VAK and meta-programmes? What is he/she?

- ▶ visual ☐
- ▶ auditory ☐
- ▶ kinaesthetic ☐
- ▶ 'towards' or 'away from' ☐
- ▶ small chunk or big chunk ☐
- ▶ match or mismatch ☐
- ▶ choices or process ☐
- ▶ internally or externally referenced ☐

How will it make a difference knowing this? Do you understand now why sometimes you don't seem to communicate? Maybe when you match their preference the communication will improve?

Your partner will have their own limiting beliefs and their own values and identity. Work out what these are and you will better understand their way of perceiving their world. Step into their shoes and be curious about this. Sometimes we can only see a situation from our own viewpoint, but, remember 'the map is not the territory'.

Focus on what is working in your relationship. We often find ourselves focusing on what is not working and feel frustrated, yet the chances are that you are overlooking all the things that work well. Think about what happens when it is going well: what is the pattern? What is the structure? Learn from the good bits and transfer the learning so you can apply it to areas that need improvement.

Modelling is a great way to develop your relationship. What does your partner do well that you could benefit from?

▶ Step 1. Think about a skill they have that you'd like.

▶ Step 2. Ask them to show you how they do it and talk you through the process.

▶ Step 3. Have a go and ask them to notice whether you are doing it exactly as they do. Make any adjustments necessary.

▶ Step 4. Ask them what they believe about this thing they do well and take on this belief for yourself.

Your body language communicates all the time. What are you saying with your body? How could you demonstrate your feelings by touch and by how you are with them?

If you always do what you've always done you will always get what you've always got. If something isn't working in your relationship, instead of nagging your partner to change, make the change yourself. Try a different approach. What would you like to change about your partner?

I'd like to change the way he/she:

_____

_____

_____

_____

_____

What could you do differently to bring about this change?

_____

_____

_____

_____

_____

How could you model the change you want in your partner?

_____

_____

_____

_____

_____

Is the drama triangle relevant? Which are you, victim, rescuer or persecutor? Maybe all three at different times? Get out of the triangle by applying what you've learned and allowing him/her to take responsibility.

Use your anchoring skills to control your state and be calm and resourceful. You can effect the change that makes the difference in your relationship.

Lastly, share what you've learned in this book. Learning and changing together can be a very loving experience.

SPORTSPEOPLE

Whatever sport you do, how you think will affect how you play. Mind and body are one. The difference between a good shot and a bad one is all about the thought process. When you stand there at the tee thinking, 'I hope this isn't a rubbish shot' it surely will be because you have an 'away from' goal and you're probably dwelling on the bad shot you made from that tee last week.

Think instead about all the great shots you've made from that tee, all the aces you've served to that player, the sixes you've hit against that cricket team and so on. Anchoring good performance is extremely useful, so when you play well, anchor it. You can use different anchors for different sports and different situations. Some people use 'lucky bands' and they work like anchors. Others have lucky shoes or shorts and they too are anchors.

Stay in the present and use 'towards' goals rather than dwelling on previous bad shots or poor games. Set a compelling outcome for each game and work towards it. Be specific about your goal, so instead of 'I'm going to play well' say 'I'm aiming for a par 3 on that hole' or 'I'm aiming to keep that ball away from our end of the pitch'. Compelling outcomes are appropriate not only for a game but even at the stroke or hit level.

> ### Case study
>
> In hockey, when doing a hit out I might be thinking about where exactly and to whom I am going to hit that ball. When I succeed it goes 'in the bank' as a success to be anchored and stored up to aid my confidence next time. If it doesn't and, after all, I can't control who will run into the space between me and the person I'm hitting to, then I learn from it and, next time, I'll make sure that person is well out of the way!

Think too about how your self-esteem varies across the course of a match. Do you start out strong and then get deflated when you lose a few points or hit some poor shots? Note this below and record your level of self-esteem at each stage as a score between 1 and 10 in the box alongside.

▶ Before the game I feel:

_____

▶ At first I feel:

_____

▶ Halfway through it I feel:

_____

▶ At the end I feel:

_____

How are you going to tackle this? You could just repeat the strategy every game, of course, or you could move out of your comfort zone, use the techniques in this book to anchor strong performance and use feedback in a positive way. Make a note below of what you could do differently next time to get a more favourable self-esteem level throughout.

_____

_____

_____

_____

_____

Feedback is essential, so use the feedback sandwich to take the learning for yourself and others to whom you give feedback: 'I played well today; I need to make my first serve much stronger overall, but it was a good game'. Try that out now, thinking about the last sporting activity you took part in.

▶ I was pleased with how it went because:

_____

_____

_____

▶ What could have been better was:

_____

_____

_____

▶ Overall I did well because:

_____

_____

_____

Many of us give up before we've even started, finding reasons why we can't go to the gym this evening, or why we can't go running. That's fine, they may be realistic reasons, but when they result in you feeling a failure or having low self-esteem then they aren't doing you any good. You need to look at what positive intention you are fulfilling by not going. In some way there is a benefit for you not exercising, otherwise you would prioritize it.

Do you value yourself? I hope you do now after reading this book. When you value yourself you will also value your health and fitness. Increasing your exercise helps in all sports so think about your identity: are you a sportsperson? Are you fit and active? If so, be who you are throughout the day, not just for the duration of the sport. Take opportunities to eat healthy food and exercise whenever you can.

Use your knowledge of VAK and the meta-programmes to help you with your training. If you are visual, then focus on what you can see. If you are auditory, focus on what you can hear and if you are kinaesthetic, focus on what you are doing and feeling. Take opportunities to disassociate and look objectively at how you are playing. Ask for feedback from your team; use internal referencing too in order to assess how well you are doing in relation to your capabilities rather than comparing yourself with others.

Case study

I find cycling uphill extremely difficult, and even though I generally have high self-esteem I have to work much harder with it in this context. I watch everyone else go up 'better' than me and I look at the seemingly endless hill. Hang on though! I am auditory. Therefore this strategy is bound to fail, isn't it, because it is visual. Therefore what I do is count the pedal strokes out loud and listen to the sound of the pedals going round and the tyres on the ground. I only look down at the road just a few centimetres beyond the front wheel. I do the same thing when I am running, I focus on the sound of my trainers and the sounds around me rather than the distance I still have to run.

What are your limiting beliefs around sport and where have they come from? You have all the skills now to recognize when one of these beliefs rears its ugly head. Recognize these 'I can'ts' as what they are: limiting. They are not helpful so choose now to take on resourceful beliefs that serve you better.

Exercise 67

Imagine you are dumping a limiting belief. Send it a text saying why you don't want it in your life, how much happier you will be without it and what you will do now that it's gone. Write it in the mobile phone screen below.

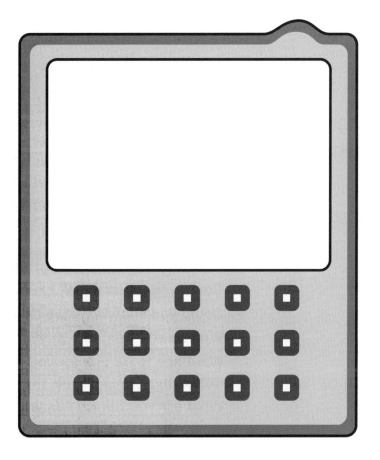

You can learn a lot from others, as well as from yourself, as you transfer skills from one area of your life to where you need them now in your sport, but also, by watching those with a skill you want, you can model their skill and take on their belief about it. Let me tell you how to do this.

Exercise 68

▶ Step 1. Think of the exact skill you want from another sportsperson and write it down here:

▷ 'I want to be able to _____

_____

_____

the way _____ does it.'

▷ Be precise because it may only be a very small part of someone's game you want to model.

▶ Step 2. Watch them do it again and again and copy exactly what they do with all the movements the same. Are you getting the result you want?

▶ Step 3. If you are then, fine, you've got it, but usually we need to ask them some questions to really get the skill. Ask:

▷ How do you do this thing I want to model?

▷ Could you talk me through it?

▷ Could you show me step by step?

▷ Why do you do it this way?

▷ What has to be true for you to get those results every time?

▷ What are you thinking as you do it?

▶ Step 4. Now ask them to watch you do it and ask them if they notice anything different in what they do that you haven't included.

▶ Step 5. A good model is one that works and that you can pass on to someone else, so have a go.

....

Use the SWISH method to change your perceptions of either teams you usually find a challenge or difficult sporting situations. Reframe them as something you will enjoy, a challenge that is well within your capability.

You will find the Logical Levels of Change (see Chapter 3) very useful as a sportsperson because it is relatively easy to pinpoint which belief you need to change to achieve your compelling outcome. Look then at the skills you need to have in order to hold that belief and check where you have them already because you DO have them. Reassess your identity, because when you change a belief the chances are you will also need to check this out with your identity and your values. Then follow on down to look at what changes in your behaviour and environment need to be made in order to be aligned.

Case study

Michael wanted to play golf every weekend but his wife thought this was rather unfair as she was left with the kids. His belief was that by playing more he would become better, but he valued his family so his beliefs and values were out of alignment. He realized though that if he were to teach his son golf and take him with him, he would be able to align them, and this is what they do now every Saturday!

Listen to feedback and use it. When one of your team says you played well, find out 'in what way?' You can do this by offering them that level of detail in your own feedback to them so they get the idea. You can also ask specifically for feedback by saying, 'I'm working on my backhand at the moment, please could you notice whether I'm following through each shot?', or whatever you're working on in your sport.

As you do your sport, notice how well you're doing it and anchor your successes so you have that high self-esteem whenever you need it.

WORK

Although there have been many examples of work situations throughout the book, it should be mentioned that, whatever work you do (whether it be office-based or not), you will need healthy self-esteem. The challenging financial climate we are currently experiencing means that no-one's job is secure.

Arguably you may need even more self-esteem to manage periods of unemployment when you are looking for a job. It's difficult to have high self-esteem when you are out of work. Look at the logical levels and use them to stay in alignment whatever the change at the environment level. You can still do things every day that will be aligned to your identity of being a working person, by keeping up to date with what's happening in your industry, networking and applying for jobs.

If you are lucky enough to have a job, and one you enjoy, maintaining good self-esteem can still be a challenge unless you apply what you've learned in this book. Focus on what is going well and check internally that you are pleased with your performance rather than expecting others to notice your excellent work. Take pride in using your skills and transferring them from one task to another.

There will always be stressful times in any industry and anchoring will be very useful to manage your state and keep you calm and resourceful. Equally, when you are asked to do something challenging or unfamiliar you can think about where you have that skill and apply it there. Use modelling to acquire the skills of others by finding out what specific skills other people use and what beliefs they hold that enable them to do that thing well.

In a work context you could model yourself on someone who sells successfully, someone who negotiates well, a good presenter and so on. Tell them that you want to model yourself on them; people are usually flattered and happy to help. They may even say there is something you do that they'd like to copy. Be curious about how they do what they do and wonder what belief you would have to have to be able to do that thing as well as they do.

Exercise 69

▶ Step 1. Note the thing you want to emulate.

▷ 'I want to copy the way: _____

_____

does _____

_____ .'

▶ Step 2. Watch and learn. Note every step of the process and every aspect: what you observe, hear and what they actually do.

▶ Step 3. Try it out for yourself and, for anything that isn't quite working as you'd like, ask them for their input.

▶ Step 4. Ask them what they are thinking at each stage and take on those beliefs for yourself.

▶ Step 5. Keep at it until you have the model and could pass it on to your colleagues.

In a company training environment, you can surely imagine how powerful a tool this can be where you select exemplars of different management skills who can pass on their model to others.

Drama triangles are just as common at work as they are in families, so watch out for rescuers and take responsibility for your own work and career. Persecutors are victims in disguise, so again keep clear of the drama triangle by recognizing it for what it is and don't allow yourself to get drawn into it. It is ultimately more respectful to allow people to rescue themselves. Can you identify each of these roles in your workplace?

► Who is a rescuer? _____

► Who is a victim? _____

► Who is a persecutor? _____

How can you ensure you don't get drawn into this triangle?

_____

_____

_____

_____

_____

Reframing can be very useful in the work environment, so if there are parts of your job you don't relish, reframe them. Lots of frequent business travellers hate travelling because they don't get to see anything other than another office in another country. You have choices. Find out more about the country you're visiting, learn a few useful phrases, food that is typical of the region and suggest meetings in local restaurants or an outing to a place of interest.

VAK and the meta-programmes will be essential tools to use in the workplace and your knowledge of how you and your colleagues operate will ensure you build rapport in your work-life. Remember, the nature of your presentations should reflect all three preferences so make them visual, auditory and kinaesthetic to get everyone engaged.

Chapter 6, on body language, should have given you the opportunity to really think about how you communicate through what you wear and how you hold yourself. Now might be a good time to reassess your wardrobe and consider how you want to be perceived, remembering that people will have formed an opinion about you based on your physical appearance before you've said a word!

If you are a student thinking about the work environment, and looking for a job, perhaps then all these aspects of self-esteem will be very relevant.

Summary

Whatever your walk of life, remember that if you always do what you've always done you will always get what you've always got. If you want high self-esteem, use the tools and techniques in this workbook to get it and keep it. It's you that has to change, not other people. Every situation, every interaction, has the opportunity for you to raise your self-esteem and for you to allow others to do so too; so take them and use them with the new knowledge that you have now.

Index

Notes

Notes

Notes